FA CUP GIANT KILLERS

FA CUP GIANT KILLERS

PAUL HARRISON

Acknowledgements

A book covering nearly 150 clubs could not be achieved without the grateful help of the various clubs and their supporters, who filled in numerous gaps once I had used my own collection. Unfortunately, the many individuals are too numerous to mention but they all know how grateful I am for their help. Thanks also to PA Photos for their help and, as usual, Tempus Publishing for taking the project on.

Frontispiece: George Harris of Cambridge is sandwiched by Tony Gibson and Ken Gray of Enfield.

First published 2007

STADIA is an imprint of
Tempus Publishing
Cirencester Road, Chalford
Stroud, Gloucestershire, GL6 8PE
www.tempus-publishing.com

© Paul Harrison, 2007

The right of Paul Harrison to be identified as the Author
of this work has been asserted in accordance with the
Copyrights, Designs and Patents Act 1988.

British Library Cataloguing in Publication Data.
A catalogue record for this book is available from the British Library.

ISBN 978 0 7524 4436 9

Typesetting and origination by NPI Media Group
Printed in Great Britain

Contents

About the Author

Paul Harrison was born in Gravesend in 1942 and has lived in the town all his life. He was educated at Dover Road Primary and Northfleet Secondary School. He is a long-time supporter of Gravesend & Northfleet FC, where he was involved for many years as programme editor and in various offices of the supporters' association. His love of grass-roots football also saw him involved for many years with the Gravesend Boys Football League. His love of both football and history has seen him write several books on the game and this is his sixth book. The first was *Southern League Post War Years* (1987), followed by *Southern League: The First Fifty Years* (1990), an updated version of *Southern League Football: The Post War Years* (1992), *Cup Glory* (1995), *Gravesend & Northfleet FC Golden Jubilee Book* (1996) and, for Tempus Publishing, *Gravesend & Northfleet FC* (2006).

Introduction

This book has been written as a tribute to the many giantkillers of non-League football – 145 to be precise – in the period covered, which is from 1925 to 2007. They have greatly enriched the competition – rightly regarded as the most famous domestic football competition in the world – without, in most cases, getting the credit for their achievements.

Once they were all part-timers and were the legendary butcher, baker and candlestick maker. These days they are more likely to be full-time players, or personal fitness trainers and computer technicians, but it is still a very difficult task to beat a Football League club simply because the influx of foreign players has pushed good-quality home-born players further down the leagues.

The famous competition was first discussed at an FA council meeting on 20 July 1871. The seven members who turned up for that meeting at the offices of *The Sportsman* on Ludgate Hill are, like the building and magazine, long gone but their decision that day to unanimously pass the proposal 'That it is desirable that a challenge cup should be established in connection with the association for which all clubs belonging to the association should be invited to compete' lives on.

The rules were drafted at the next meeting and the competition was ready for the 1871/72 season, culminating in The Wanderers beating Royal Engineers at the Oval in front of a modest crowd of 2,000. Ironically, two of those committee members who launched the competition played major roles in that first final, with Morton Betts firing past Francis Maradin in the Engineers' goal!

Few would have expected after that modest start that by the turn of the century the gate would be into six figures. One of the reasons for this was that Southern League Tottenham Hotspur had caught the public imagination on their way to the 1901 final, where they took on one of the giants of the day – Sheffield United – who were able to field nine internationals. The underdogs won in a replay that still rates as the greatest ever giantkilling, although Tottenham were very much a team on the up and within a few brief years were members of the Football League themselves. Southampton, another non-League side, had lost out narrowly the previous year and in 1910 Swindon were beaten at the semi-final stage in the last strong challenge by a Southern League club.

The best non-Leaguers were quickly snapped up as the Football League expanded and a major change was needed in the competition in 1925 to enable the minnows to come into their own again, six rather than four rounds in the competition proper providing the opportunity for thirty-two non-Leaguers to play at the first-round stage. This provided the stage for a whole new era of clubs progressing through the ranks to the Football League, like Carlisle, Mansfield and Ipswich via headline-grabbing cup runs. After the Second World War this was repeated by Colchester, Gillingham, Scunthorpe and Shrewsbury, and later still by Peterborough and Hereford, although the most famous of all giantkillers, Yeovil, did it via promotion from the Conference following the instigation of automatic promotion and relegation in 1986.

With a swish new Wembley the venue for the culmination of a competition that starts each August and ends the following May, the FA Cup is as popular as ever, and one of the vital ingredients is the non-League giantkiller, let no one forget it.

Key to Abbreviations

AL	Athenian League
APL	Alliance Premier League
BL	Birmingham League
CC	Cheshire Combination
CL	Cheshire League
CON	Conference
ECL	Eastern Counties League
FL1	Football League First Division
FL2	Football League Second Division
FL3	Football League Third Division
FL3N	Football League Third Division (North)
FL3S	Football League Third Division (South)
FL4	Football League Fourth Division
HL	Hampshire League
IL	Isthmian League
KL	Kent League
LC	Lancashire Combination
ML	Midlands League
NC	Notts Combination
NCL	Northern Counties League
NEL	North Eastern League
NL	Northern League
NPL	Northern Premier League
NRL	North Regional League
SL	Southern League
WL	Welsh League
WMRL	West Midlands Regional League

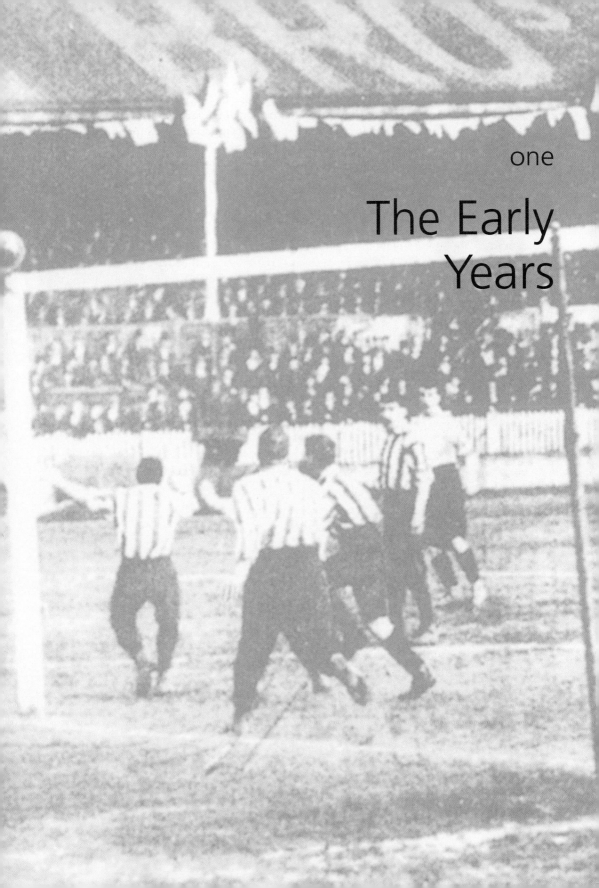

one

The Early Years

When the FA Cup began in 1872, the term non-League did not exist for the rather obvious reason that no leagues had yet been formed. This would all change with the introduction of the twelve-team Football League in 1888, which creamed off the fast-improving and ambitious sides from the North and Midlands who quickly dominated the competition.

The first non-League side to reach the FA Cup final were Football Alliance side Sheffield Wednesday in 1890 when they were crushed 6-1 at the Oval by the might of Blackburn Rovers, who collected the trophy for a fourth time. In 1892 The Alliance became the Second Division of the Football League and it was left to the Southern League, formed in 1894, to make a strong threat to the Football League's dominance. At this stage only one club from the Football League – Woolwich Arsenal – came from the south of the country and it took the rest of the decade to mount the expected threat, but when it came it was a formidable one.

It proved to be a golden spell for non-League, and the Southern League in particular, as Southampton in 1900 and 1902, and Tottenham Hotspur famously in 1901 reached the final. The Saints were crushed 4-0 by Bury in the 1900 final but Spurs fared better as the side captured the public imagination and attracted the cup's first six-figure attendance, 110,820 packing the Crystal Palace to see them take on the then mighty Sheffield United – it was the largest crowd recorded at any football match at the time. Despite fielding nine internationals, the Blades were fortunate to gain a 2-2 draw with a controversial goal to equalise when the referee – far from play – ruled Spurs' goalkeeper George Clawley had dropped the ball over his goal line, despite the better-placed linesman making no such claim.

Despite seemingly losing their best chance, Spurs again had the better of the replay and this time were not to be denied, winning 3-1 at Burnden Park, with Sandy Brown scoring the clinching goal to complete the achievement of scoring in each round.

The following season Sheffield United again had Southern League opposition in Southampton and once again the first match was drawn – this time 1-1 – but the replay saw them narrowly beat the non-Leaguers 2-1. It was the last appearance of a non-League side in the final, although four more times Southern Leaguers would reach the semi-finals – Millwall (1903), Southampton (1908) and Swindon (1910 and 1912) – each time suffering the heartbreak of exiting at the penultimate stage.

Soon war clouds would gather and like everything else football would never be the same again. In 1920 the Football League took the top division of the Southern League to form a Third Division, and a year later a further division was introduced to enable a Third Division (South) and Third Division (North) to be created. The Football League had grown from twelve to eighty-eight clubs and the role of non-League sides in the famous competition had been pushed to the fringes. Not only that, but in the early 1920s, with just four rounds and a semi-final in the competition proper, many Football League clubs were bowing out in the qualifying competition and non-Leaguers were being snuffed out without a mention. Something had to change and after much discussion the FA Cup committee came up with a system that has stood the test of time. Instead of four rounds in the competition proper, it would be six rounds with a mix of Third Division and non-League sides making up the first two rounds, and the forty-four sides from the top two divisions entering at the third round.

So once more the non-League sides, now much lower down the pyramid than in the early days, would have a chance to make their mark, and how they did so is what this book is about.

In 1900 Southampton became the first Southern League team to reach the FA Cup final and, indeed, the first side from the South to reach that stage since 1883. Unfortunately for the Saints, they came up against a Bury side on top of their game and a 68,945 crowd at Crystal Palace saw the First Division team win 4-0. This photo shows a rare attack from the striped Saints.

A world-record crowd of 110,820 wait in anticipation on 20 April 1901 at Crystal Palace as First Division aces Sheffield United prepare to kick off against Southern Leaguers Tottenham, who had captured the nation's heart with a sensational run. The high attendance underlined the popularity of a competition that had seen a crowd of just 2,000 for the first final in 1872 – only twenty-nine years earlier.

Sandy Brown became the first player to score in each round of the cup and is seen in the centre of this picture again causing problems for the Sheffield United defence as Tottenham bid to make history at Crystal Palace in a 2-2 draw. Their date with history would have to wait for a week.

Although the two greatest defenders of the era, Ernest 'Nudger' Needham and Bill 'Fatty' Foulke, bar his way, Sandy Brown (only his arm can be seen) is about to glance in a header to make it 3-1 and give Tottenham a memorable and unique cup win. They were the only non-League side to lift the trophy – a feat that will almost certainly never be repeated. For Sheffield United there were no complaints as they were very much second best in the Burnden Park, Bolton replay.

Opposite above left: Alex 'Sandy' Brown. The Beith-born Scot was the key component in Spurs' memorable cup run, scoring in every round, including all four against West Brom in the semi-final. The centre forward also played for Preston, Portsmouth and Middlesbrough.

Opposite above right: Charles Burgess Fry (1872-1956). The legendary C.B. was an amazing all-round sportsman and whilst he was best known for his cricketing prowess, playing for England in eight Ashes series, he was also a fine rugby player for Harlequins and top full-back for Southampton, playing in their two clashes with Sheffield United in the 1902 final. Just for good measure, he was the world long-jump record holder at the time of the first Olympics in 1896 and when asked years later why he wasn't among the finalists in Athens for the long-jump competition, he had a unique, if amazing, excuse: 'I didn't go as I was unaware they were taking place.'

Opposite below: The history-making Tottenham side line up at the start of the historic 1900/01 season with the Southern League Championship – the prelude to their historic FA Cup win of 1900/01.

Southampton just failed to equal the achievement of Tottenham the following year when they too faced Sheffield United and took them to a replay before losing 2-1 in a game captured in the popular cartoon form of the day.

two

The 1920s

The non-League triumphs of the 1920s were well spread between fourteen clubs, with Rhyl from the Welsh League leading the way with a trio of victims. Two fast-improving and ambitious sides – Carlisle United of the North Eastern League and Mansfield Town of the Midland League – collected two scalps, as did Corinthians, who were unattached to any league and were exempt from the first two rounds, despite much criticism by other senior non-League sides. But they did justify this with hammerings of Walsall and Norwich on their own grounds, a narrow defeat to Millwall after three games, and solid performances against giants of the period Manchester City and Newcastle United.

The most successful league during the period was the Midland League with six victories. Closely behind were the North Eastern League with five wins, the Welsh League with four, the Southern League with three, and the Athenian, Isthmian and Kent Leagues with one apiece.

The twenty-three Football League victims were surprisingly well spread with eighteen different clubs suffering, Hartlepools leading the way with four defeats in the five completed seasons. The only other clubs to suffer more than one defeat were Norwich City and Queens Park Rangers who suffered two.

The general opinion that the Third Division (North) was weaker than the South was given weight by the fact that fifteen defeats were inflicted on sides from the North as opposed to only seven from the South with a single Second Division side – Wolves – making up the number.

Giantkillers of the 1920s

(Non-League sides in capitals)

Season	Round					
1925/26	1	CLAPTON (IL)	3	Norwich City (FL3S)	1
	1	WORKSOP TOWN (ML)	1	Coventry City (FL3N)	0
	1R	BLYTH SPARTANS (NEL)	2	Hartlepools (FL3N)	1
	2	BOSTON TOWN (ML)	1	Bradford PA (FL3N)	0
	2R	Rochdale (FL3N)	1	CHILTON COLLIERY (NEL)	2
1926/27	1	CARLISLE UNITED (NEL)	6	Hartlepools (FL3N)	2
	1	POOLE TOWN (SL)	1	Newport County (FL3N)	0
	1R	RHYL (WL)	2	Stoke City (FL3N)	1
	2	RHYL (WL)	3	Wrexham (FL3N)	1
	3	Walsall (FL3N)	0	CORINTHIANS	4
1927/28	1	ALDERSHOT (SL)	2	Queens Park Rangers (FL3S)	1
	1	CARLISLE UNITED (NEL)	2	Doncaster Rovers (FL3N)	1
	1	RHYL (WL)	4	Wigan Borough (FL3N)	3
1928/29	1	GAINSBOROUGH TRINITY (ML)	3	Crewe Alexandra (FL3N)	1
	1	GUILDFORD CITY (SL)	4	Queens Park Rangers (FL3S)	2
	1	SPENNYMOOR UNITED (NEL)	5	Hartlepools (FL3N)	1
	2	Barrow (FL3N)	1	MANSFIELD TOWN (ML)	2
	3	Wolves (FL2)	0	MANSFIELD TOWN (ML)	2
	3	Norwich City (FL3S)	0	CORINTHIAN	5
1929/30	1	CAERNARFON TOWN (WL)	4	Darlington (FL3N)	2
	1	Gillingham (FL3S)	0	MARGATE (KL)	2
	1	LEYTON (AL)	4	Merthyr Town (FL3S)	1
	1	SCUNTHORPE UNITED (ML)	1	Hartlepools (FL3N)	0

A.G. Bower

Alf Bower (1895–1970). The Bromley-born full-back gave outstanding service to Corinthians during the 1920s and was good enough to play five times for England at full international level.

Benjamin Howard-Baker (1892-1987). The Liverpool-born goalkeeper was another of Corinthian's outstanding crop of players in the 1920s. He also played as an amateur for Chelsea and Everton.

The programme for Corinthian's fourth-round clash with First Division leaders Newcastle. The game attracted 56,338 people to Crystal Palace and Newcastle eventually won through 3-1 after trailing 1-0 at the interval. The match was broadcast live on the radio – the first FA Cup tie to get this treatment just a week after the first ever football broadcast of the First Division game between Arsenal and Sheffield United.

Norman Creek (1898-1980). Creek was born in Darlington and was one of a rare breed to win the Military Cross and score a goal in the FA Cup competition proper. Following his heroics in the First World War, he became a mainstay of the Corinthians side as a centre forward, later writing a history on the club and managing the England amateur side.

Chilton Colliery were one of many mining sides who entered the competition but were the only giantkillers when in 1925/26 they beat Rochdale at Spotland after a 1-1 draw at home. They had already beaten Carlisle 2-0 at Brunton Park but hopes of a third-round glamour tie were dashed by a trip to Second Division South Shields where they lost 3-0. The mine was situated seven miles south of Durham and operated between 1872 and 1966.

CHILTON WIN WITH TEN MEN

Amateurs' Amazing Triumph in Second Round Cup Replay at Rochdale.

CENTRE-HALF ORDERED OFF THE FIELD BEFORE THE INTERVAL.

Chilton Colliery, the plucky amateur side, thoroughly merited their win over Rochdale by two goals to one, in the F.A Cup replay on the Spotland Heights, yesterday, although the result was probably as big a surprise to them as it was to Rochdale.

It was the most sensational Cup-tie defeat the Rochdale club have suffered during the whole of their career, for it was fully expected that Chilton would be outclassed in the replay.

Chilton Show The Way.

Not once during the game were Chilton in arrears, and their victory was all the more praiseworthy because they played throughout the second half with only 10 men, Catterick being ordered off the field just before the interval.

Although operating against the wind and the drizzling rain in the first half Chilton opened the scoring after only 10 minutes' play, MARTIN putting the finishing touch to a centre by Scurr. In further play they were extremely dangerous, but later Rochdale showed more determination, and after 40 minutes they equalised, PARKES scoring direct from a free kick awarded against Catterick.

In this instance Catterick was cautioned, but he was unlucky to be made the scapegoat in a fairly rough game by being sent off a couple of minutes later for a further offence.

After the interval Chilton put Winter at centre-half for Catterick, and with the visitors' attack weakened it looked as though Rochdale would secure a runaway victory, but this was not to be. Although Rochdale attacked almost continually they encountered a smart defence, Guthrie distinguished himself by making some wonderful saves. To Guthrie for his remarkable clearances Chilton undoubtedly

A. THOMPSON.

owed a tremendous debt of gratitude. Eight minutes from the end, with Rochdale in the visitors' half, Dunn broke away, and from his inside pass THOMPSON won the game for the Amateurs, with a long dropping shot, the ball rebounding off the far post into the net.

To Meet South Shields.

Rochdale tried desperately to get on terms again, but were kept at bay. The attendance was disappointing, being only 1,500, and the receipts £60.

Chilton have thus qualified to meet South Shields, at Horsley Hill, in the third round, and their visit will be eagerly awaited after their sensational performance at Rochdale, which emphasised the dour Cup-fighting qualities of the Colliers.

James McConnell (1899-1949). Born in Ayr, McConnell was a bustling centre forward who helped Carlisle into the Football League after playing for Kilmarnock and Celtic. He scored the winning goal for the then North Eastern Leaguers to tip Doncaster Rovers out of the 1927/28 FA Cup and put them on the way to a Football League place at the end of the season.

Above left: Alexander Doggart (1897-1963). Bishop Auckland-born Doggart was another player from the golden age of Corinthians, scoring in several key matches including the 5-0 thrashing of Norwich City at Carrow Road in 1929. A skilful inside forward, he later became a key administrator in the game, rising to become chairman of the Football Association, a role he held when he collapsed and died at the 1963 AGM of the Football Association.

Above right: Spennymoor United were one of four non-League teams to knock Hartlepools United out of the FA Cup in the 1920s.

Frank Hoddinott

Left: Frank Hoddinott (1894–1980). The Welshman, born at Brecon, had a long Football League career at Chelsea, Crystal Palace and Watford before in the twilight of his career playing a major role from inside forward in Rhyl's fine cup runs of the 1920s.

Below: The Scunthorpe team that beat Hartlepool, from left to right, back row: Severn, Skull, Bromage, Cooke, Bailey, Daynham. Front row: Simmons, Stringfellow, Smalley, Calladine, Beynon.

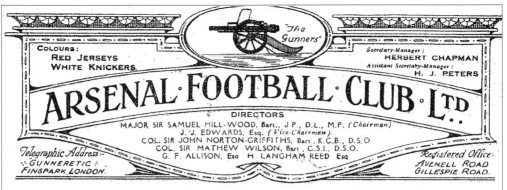

COLOURS:
RED JERSEYS
WHITE KNICKERS.

"The Gunners"

Secretary-Manager:
HERBERT CHAPMAN
Assistant Secretary-Manager:
H. J. PETERS

ARSENAL·FOOTBALL·CLUB·L.T.D.

DIRECTORS
MAJOR SIR SAMUEL HILL-WOOD, Bart., J.P., D.L., M.P. (Chairman)
J. J. EDWARDS, Esq. (Vice-Chairmen).
COL. SIR JOHN NORTON-GRIFFITHS, Bart., K.C.B., D.S.O
COL. SIR MATHEW WILSON, Bart., C.S.I., D.S.O.
G. F. ALLISON, Esq. H. LANGHAM REED Esq.

Telegraphic Address:
GUNNERETIC
FINSPARK, LONDON.

Registered Office
AVENELL ROAD
GILLESPIE ROAD.

Vol. XVII. No. 26.   Saturday, January 26th, 1929.   Two-Pence.

ARSENAL v. MANSFIELD TOWN
F.A. CUP, 4th ROUND.

OUR EDITORIAL NOTE
BY "LANCEJACK."

WELCOME, Mansfield Town! Since the gallant little Nottinghamshire club made history by knocking Wolverhampton Wanderers out of the Cup a fortnight ago they have basked in the sunshine of kind publicity. So many nice things have appeared in print about their officials and their players that everyone connected with the club has been in grave danger of having his head turned by praise. Their record is indeed an amazing one for they have arrived at the Fourth Round of the Cup after playing through the qualifying stages and playing each of their last four ties away from home. They have knocked out a Third Division (Northern Section) club in Barrow and a Second Division club in the Wolves. To-day comes the greatest test of all. Whatever their fate at Highbury these Mansfield lads will always be able to look back on the present season with justifiable pride.

Team That Cost Nothing.

For an obscure team suddenly to rise and deal a shattering blow at one of the League clubs, as Mansfield Town did a fortnight ago at the Molineux Grounds is not new but it is a very rare happening in these days and their achievement takes rank with the best that have ever been accomplished in the Cup. And here are three facts which must cause those who are responsible for the running of first-class clubs furiously to think: not a farthing was spent in signing on the players who will represent Mansfield at Highbury this afternoon, not a penny was spent in summer wages, and the weekly wages bill of the team that beat the Wolves does not exceed £38. Cup-tie history simply teems with surprise and romance but nothing quite so dramatic as the rise to fame of this Midland League side has ever been known. They come to town to-day as the sole survivors of the Nottinghamshire clubs.

Good Cup Fighters.

It was only two years before the War that Mansfield Town came into existence and not until the club was formed into a limited liability com-

Above, below and previous page: Mansfield Town were formed in 1910 and made a big impact in 1928/29 as members of the Midland League by beating Shirebrook, Barrow and then Wolves at Molineaux. The Stags then went to Highbury to take on Arsenal and produced another fine show before going down to two late goals. Continued good form saw them elected to the Football League in 1931.

three

The 1930s

Almost a full decade was played out despite a serious economic situation and an ever more turbulent world situation. The nine seasons saw a total of thirty-eight giantkillings. The most successful side of the period were Workington, who took four scalps (including three in 1933/34); not far behind were Scarborough, Gainsborough and the emerging Yeovil & Petters United – to be known from 1946 by the more familiar name of Yeovil Town – with three victories.

A pair of victories were also achieved by Kent teams Folkestone and Margate, whilst Midland Leaguers Scunthorpe United achieved the same success. Playing in their first season, Chelmsford City did likewise in a march to the fourth round in the last season of the decade.

Despite a loss of members during the depression, the Southern League, with its knack of providing up-and-coming teams, led the way with fifteen victories. The Midland League with ten and North Eastern League with five followed in their wake, while the Cheshire League had three wins. Five other Leagues attained one victory each: the Athenian League, Birmingham League, Isthmian League, Lancashire Combination and Notts Combination.

Although the Third Division (North) again suffered the most casualties among the non-Leaguers with nineteen, it was a close run thing with the Third Division (South) suffering only one less, the tally completed by Second Division Southampton.

War clouds were gathering when the 1939/40 competition began with the extra preliminary round on 2 September 1939. The following morning Prime Minister Neville Chamberlain made his famous speech declaring war with Germany and football suddenly didn't seem important anymore. As the country began six long years of war, football and the FA Cup took a back seat.

Giantkillers of the 1930s

(Non-League sides in capitals)

Season	Round					
1930/31	I	NEWARK TOWN (ML)	2	Rotherham United (FL3N)	I
	2	Gillingham (FL3S)	I	ALDERSHOT (SL)	3
	2	SCARBOROUGH (ML)	6	Lincoln City (FL3N)	4
1931/32	I	CROOK TOWN (NEL)	3	Stockport County (FL3N)	I
	I	SCUNTHORPE UNITED (ML)	3	Rochdale (FL3N)	I
	IR	GAINSBOROUGH TRINITY (ML)	I	Crewe Alexandra (FL3N)	0
	2	BATH CITY (SL)	2	Crystal Palace (FL3S)	I
	2	BURTON TOWN (BL)	4	Gateshead (FL3N)	I
	2	DARWEN (LC)	2	Chester (FL3N)	I
1932/33	I	FOLKESTONE (SL)	I	Norwich City (FL3S)	0
	I	York City (FL3N)	I	SCARBOROUGH (ML)	3
	2	FOLKESTONE (SL)	2	Newport County (FL3S)	I
1933/34	I	SUTTON TOWN (NC)	2	Rochdale (FL3N)	I
	I	WORKINGTON (NEL)	I	Southport (FL3N)	0
	2	Carlisle United (FL3N)	I	CHELTENHAM (SL)	2
	2	WORKINGTON (NEL)	3	Newport County (FL3S)	I
	3	WORINGTON (NEL)	4	Gateshead (FL3N)	I
1934/35	I	Carlisle United (FL3N)	I	WIGAN ATHLETIC (CL)	6
	I	YEOVIL & PETTERS UTD (SL)	3	Crystal Palace (FL3S)	0
	2	WIGAN ATHLETIC (CL)	3	Torquay United (FL3S)	2
	2	YEOVIL & PETTERS UTD (SL)	4	Exeter City (FL3S)	I
1935/36	I	Cardiff City (FL3S)	0	DARTFORD (SL)	3
	I	MARGATE (SL)	3	Queens Park Rangers (FL3S)	I
	I	New Brighton (FL3N)	I	WORKINGTON (NEL)	3
	I	SOUTHALL (AL)	3	Swindon Town (FL3S)	I
	I	York City (FL3N)	I	BURTON TOWN (ML)	5

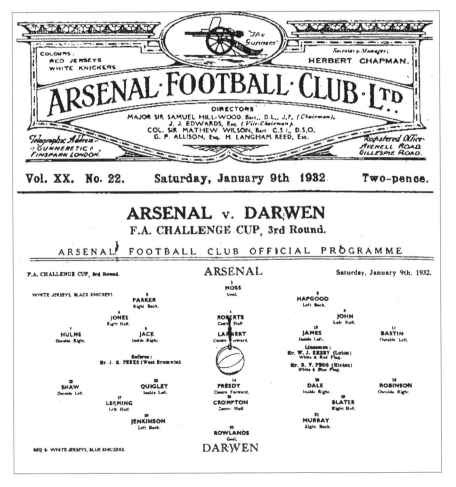

Darwen were once members of the Football League (1891-1899) but gradually faded from the top levels. They were playing in the Lancashire Combination when they had a great run in 1931/32, beating fellow non-Leaguers Peterborough & Fletton United in the first round and then the Third Division (North) side Chester 2-1 to earn a glamour tie at Arsenal, where matters went disastrously wrong as they crashed to an 11-1 defeat.

NEWARK'S TRIUMPH.

Midland Leaguers Give Rotherham the Go-By.

INJURED GRAY'S PLUCK.
(By "Westgate.")

Both teams were at full strength, F. C. Wheeler, the amateur outside-left, returning to the United's team after a week's absence, causing Murden to move from outside to inside-left.

The Midland League team included Best, who as goalkeeper for the United, was always popular with the Millmoor supporters.

There was a representative number of Rotherham, all wearing red and white colours, and the Merry Miller, the Supporters' Club mascot, was prominently placed so that it could be seen from all parts of the ground. Rain fell throughout the morning, and it was falling when the game commenced. Teams:—

Newark Town.—Best; Pearson and York; Stanniland, Bennett and Lowe; McLean, Roseboom, Steed, Hoddinott and Morton.

Rotherham United.—Harris; Jackson and Freeman; Skull, Bratley and Whitworth; Sellars, Gray, Hick, Murden and F. C. Wheeler.

Referee: Mr. Manderfield (Grantham).

The teams turned out before about 2,000 spectators. The United mascot was presented to Jackson, the captain of the team, when he went on to the field.

Jackson won the toss and took advantage of the wind. From the start Gray pushed the ball up the centre of the field to Hick, who put it out to Wheeler. The left-winger, however, lost the ball to Stanniland. On two occasions Stanniland stopped passes out to Wheeler. From the start it was evident that it was difficult to control the ball.

The first thrill was provided by Bratley, who fired over the bar. Newark attacked on the right, but the ball was put behind by McLean. A centre from Morton was dropping straight for Steed, but Freeman cleared.

After a dangerous raid by Rotherham, when a shot from Murden was smothered, Newark went down, and a centre from Morton was headed away by Freeman. The home side appealed for a goal on the grounds that the ball had been over the line. The appeal, however was ignored.

Newark were repeatedly putting the ball in the goalmouth and SPEED scored after 23 minutes.

Newark kept up the pressure and the Rotherham goal had a narrow escape when Roseboom put in a cross shot, which missed by inches.

Five minutes from half-time STEED added a second goal. Hoddinott shot in and as Harris met it he could not hold it and Steed put it into the net.

A minute later MURDEN scored for Rotherham, heading in beautifully from Sellars. Half-time:—Newark Town 2, Rotherham United 1.

Rotherham forced two corners without success. Steed was allowed to go on when apparently well offside, but Harris got to the ball first, and a foul was given for him when Steed bumped him.

The game continued to be played at a terrific speed, and considering the state of the ground it was a good game. Thrills were plentiful, Bratley trying a long shot without success.

Rotherham were coming into the picture, but the Midland Leaguers were a smart lot, and gave nothing away.

After 12 minutes Gray was carried off the field.

Whitworth put in a long shot, but was hopelessly wide.

Wheeler played pretty football before passing to Murden, but the inside man's shot was smothered.

Gray returned after five minutes' absence, but soon after he collapsed after heading the ball and was again taken off.

Rotherham were fighting desperately, and were certainly having the better of matters now. They were attacking persistently in spite of the handicap of playing with only ten men.

GRAY OFF FOR THIRD TIME.

Sellars and Wheeler did some good work. It was quite a long time before Harris was tested and that was when he cleared a centre from Morton.

Gray walked on to the field but the trainer, Mr. Slade, took him off again.

Hick put in a high shot which Best caught and cleared with his usual brilliance.

The United were exerting themselves to their fullest extent, and a shot from Sellars rested on the top of the net.

Twice from goal kicks Harris put the ball out of play.

It was undoubtedly unfortunate that Rotherham lost Gray for so long. With nine minutes to go Gray went on to the field again at outside-right. He appeared very unsteady.

Right to the end Rotherham fought with all their might. A corner by Sellars dropped dangerously in the goalmouth and was scrambled away.

Gray was beaten, but he insisted in staying on the field.

Result:—NEWARK TOWN 2
ROTHERHAM UNITED ... 1
Receipts £125; attendance 2,700.

Left: Newark Town had a rare moment in the sun with a shock victory over Third Division (North) Rotherham United. The Midland Leaguers were brought crashing down to earth in the second round, though, with a 6-0 defeat at Crystal Palace. The club were members of the Midland League (1892-1939) but never played senior-level football again.

Below: Cheltenham Town – founded in 1892 – were long-time members of the Southern League before their rise to the Football League in 1999. Their only giantkilling cup run came in 1933/34 – their first appearance in the FA Cup competition proper. They beat Barnet of the Athenian League 5-1 and then went to Third Division (North) Carlisle United and won 2-1 before losing out at their Whaddon Road ground to Second Division Blackpool 3-1. Pictured is Payne about to score Cheltenham's goal against Blackpool's striped defenders before a record near-10,000 crowd.

Billy Boyd

Formed in 1894, Workington eventually became members of the Football League from 1951 until 1977. They had a memorable run in 1933/34 as members of the North Eastern League. Ironically, they lost their place in 1976/77, failing to be re-elected – a fate the three Football League sides they had beaten in 1933/34 all suffered. Southport (1-0), Newport County (3-1) and Gateshead (4-1) were their victims, all losing at Lonsdale Park before Preston went there in the fourth round and scrambled a 2-1 win. Among the key players was Scottish centre forward Billy Boyd (1905-1967). Born in Cambuslang, the Scottish centre forward moved South after playing for Clyde. He also appeared for Manchester United and Sheffield United before becoming a mainstay in another strong cup run for Workington in 1935/36, hitting a hat-trick against Third Division (North) New Brighton in the first round and four in the second round against Kidderminster before the team lost out in the third round to Second Division Bradford Park Avenue.

Louis Page

Louis Page (1899–1959), born in Kirkdale, played a key role in the upsurge of Yeovil as player–manager in their first significant giantkilling run in 1934/35, when they crushed Third Division (South) Crystal Palace 3-0 and Exeter City 4-1 on the Huish slopes before bowing out to Liverpool 6-2.

Jack Lambert

Jack Lambert (1902-1940). Born in Greasebrough, the former Arsenal and Fulham forward finished his career at Margate. He helped the Southern Leaguers reach the third round in 1935/36, scoring in the 3-1 first-round win over QPR. Crystal Palace were beaten by the same margin in the next round before Margate lost to Second Division Blackpool again 3-1 in the third round.

DERBY COUNTY

Right Wing   Left Wing

1
Kirby

2   3
Udall   Jessop

4   5   6
Nicholas   Barker   Keen

7   8   9   10   11
Crooks   Napier   Gallacher   Ramage   Halford

Referee :—G. C. DENTON (Northampton).
Linesmen : R. V. Wood (Sheffield), Red Flag ; L. Phillips (Wolverhampton), Blue Flag.

12   13   14   15   16
Harron   Mercer   Meads   Dell   McGregor

17   18   19
L. Hunt   Nicholas   Patrick

20   21
Collins   Hogg

22
Cunningham

Left Wing.   Right Wing

DARTFORD

Above and left: Dartford produced a stunning performance to beat Cardiff City 3-0 in the first round of the 1935/36 competition at Ninian Park just eight years after the Bluebirds had become the first, and so far only, team to take the cup out of England. Gainsborough Trinity were put to the sword 4-0 in the second round. Then came a visit to the Baseball Ground to take on high-riding First Division leaders Derby County and Darts stormed into a 2-0 lead before eventually losing 3-2. Dartford were first formed in 1888 and, after losing their Watling Street ground in 1992, battled back from the bottom of the pyramid. In 2006/07 they moved into a new ground and looked set for a rosy future. This photo shows the Darts in unfamiliar stripes, with goalkeeper Cunningham punching clear.

Davie Robbie

SCUNTHORPE UNITED GET THROUGH

Above left: David Robbie (1899-1978) was born in Motherwell. The outside right also scored for Margate in the victory over QPR. After moving from Scotland he had a thirteen-year career at Bury. He also played at Manchester United and Plymouth before ending his career, like Jack Lambert, on the sunny South Coast.

Above right: Scunthorpe United of the Midland League chalked up their third giantkilling with a 4-2 victory over Third Division (South) Coventry in the first round – the same opposition who slammed them 7-0 at the same stage of the competition the previous season.

Below: Ipswich Town began their climb up the footballing ladder with a good run in the 1935/36 competition beating Watford and going on to win the Southern League Championship. From left to right, back row: Read (assistant secretary), Astill, Perrit, Thomson, Shufflebottom, Cowey, Parry, Carter, Edwards, McPherson (trainer). Middle row: Hooper (director), Williams, Bunbery, McLuckie (captain), O'Brien, Capitain Cobbold (chairman), R. Cobbold (director), Bruce, Jackson (director), Shaw (director), Allsop. Front row: Hays, Houldsworth.

Above left: Guildford City followed Ipswich as Southern League champions and also as giantkillers in 1937/38 by beating Reading of the Third Division (South) 1-0. A heavy 4-0 defeat followed in the second round away to Doncaster Rovers. Formed in 1921, Guildford City sadly folded in 1976 despite their huge potential.

Above right: Runcorn had a great run in the 1938/39 competition, with victories over Wellington and Aldershot, before losing out at Canal Street to Preston 4-2 before a record crowd of 10,112.

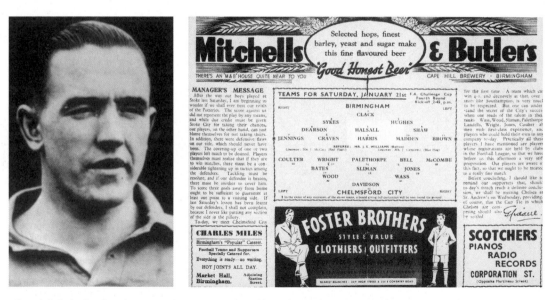

Above left: Jack Coulter (1912-1981). Born in Whiteabbey, the Irish international winger scored against both Darlington and Southampton during Chelmsford's amazing cup run in 1938/39.

Above right: Chelmsford City were formed in 1938 and must have expected a season or two of consolidation. Instead, a dramatic cup run to the fourth round proper sent the area cup crazy. Kidderminster were crushed 4-1, then came Third Division (North) Darlington 3-1 and Second Division Southampton 4-1. The Southern Leaguers finally bowed out to First Division Birmingham City 6-0 in the fourth round, but they had certainly got onto the football map much earlier than anticipated.

four

The 1940s

Just like the 1920s, only five seasons were played during the '40s due to the Second World War. When the competition began again in 1945 it was played on a two-leg basis to help offset the shortage of fixtures due to the Football League deciding not to restart until the following season. Now that games were played over two legs it was even harder for non-Leaguers to go through as the sudden-death factor was slightly changed. In fact, Newport (IOW) lost an incredible four times during the competition – a feat that will surely never be repeated. They first lost to Frome in the qualifying rounds (which were not played over two legs) but the Somerset side were thrown out for fielding an ineligible player. Then, after losing at Clapton (soon to be Leyton Orient), they overturned a 2-1 deficit only to lose both legs to Aldershot in the next round.

For the first time two non-Leaguers battled through to the fifth round and also set a precedent by beating First Division sides for the first time since the new format began in 1925.

The seventeen scalps for the non-Leaguers over five years meant the least successful batch of results yet, with the Southern League again the most successful with eleven victories. The Midland League managed three wins and there was one apiece for the North Eastern and Isthmian Leagues, as well as a first success for the Hampshire League.

Most of the successful clubs would soon be members of the Football League, with Colchester and Gillingham leading the way with a trio of victories. They and Scunthorpe, with two wins, would be elected in 1950, whilst Yeovil, who also managed two wins, would wreak havoc for a further fifty years or more!

For the first time it was good to see two First Division casualties along with a pair of defeated Second Division sides. For the first time the Third Division (South) were the chief casualties with eight whilst the Third Division (North) had a mere five.

Giantkillers of the 1940s

(Non-League sides in capitals)

Season	Round					
1945/46	1	NEWPORT (IOW) (HL)	3	Clapton Orient (FL3S)	2★
	1	LOVELLS ATHLETIC (SL)	6	Bournemouth (FL3S)	4★
	1	SHREWSBURY TOWN (ML)	6	Walsall (FL3S)	4★
1946/47	1	MERTHYR TYDFIL (SL)	3	Bristol Rovers (FL3S)	1
	1	York City (FL3N)	0	SCUNTHORPE UTD (ML)	1
	2	Bristol City (FL3S)	1	GILLINGHAM (SL)	2
1947/48	1	GILLINGHAM (SL)	1	Leyton Orient (FL3S)	0
	1	Lincoln City (FL3N)	0	WORKINGTON (NEL)	2
	2	COLCHESTER UTD (SL)	1	Wrexham (FL3N)	0
	2R	GILLINGHAM (SL)	3	Rochdale (FL3N)	0
	3	COLCHESTER UTD (SL)	1	Huddersfield Town (FL1)	0
	4	COLCHESTER UTD (SL)	3	Bradford PA (FL2)	2
1948/49	1	LEYTONSTONE (IL)	2	Watford (FL3S)	1
	1R	SCUNTHORPE UTD (ML)	1	Halifax Town (FL3N)	0
	3	YEOVIL TOWN (SL)	3	Bury (FL2)	1
	4	YEOVIL TOWN (SL)	2	Sunderland (FL1)	1
1949/50	1R	Aldershot (FL3S)	2	WEYMOUTH (SL)	3

★on aggregate

John Maund

John Maund (1916-1994) was born in Hednesford and started with his home-town team before progressing to Aston Villa. A fast, direct winger on either flank, he signed for Shrewsbury after the war and blitzed Walsall with a hat-trick in a 5-0 cup rampage. They were clearly impressed and signed him the following season.

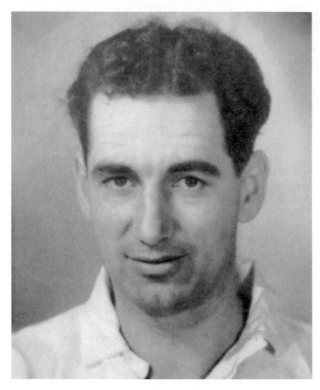

Harry Clarke (1923-2000) was born in Woodford and played a major role in Lovell Athletic's great run of 1945/46 before moving on to Tottenham, where he played nearly 300 games at centre half.

Bernard Streten (1921-1994). Born in Gillingham, the goalkeeper began his career with Shrewsbury and was a key member of the side in 1945/46. He was one of the few players to gain international honours for England at both amateur and full levels, and later played 300 games for Luton Town.

Merthyr Tydfil were one of the great non-League sides in the years 1946 to 1954. Strangely, their string of triumphs included little success in the FA Cup, besides a 1946/47 victory over Third Division (South) Bristol Rovers by a 3-1 margin. Reading dented their hopes of further progress with a 3-1 victory at Penydarren Park in the second round in front of a 19,500 crowd. The team is pictured, from left to right, back row: Billy Moore (trainer), Davies, Lowe, Reid, Pugh, Richards, Albert Lindon (manager). Middle row: Howarth, Allen, Raybould, Simpson. Front row: Avery, Hullett, Powell.

Cup fever at Merthyr in the run-up to the Bristol Rovers match.

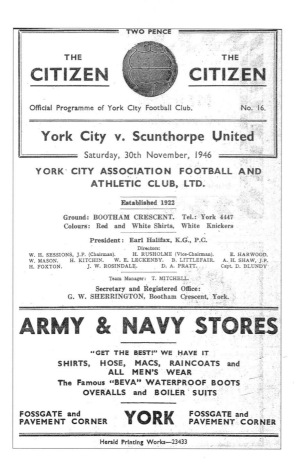

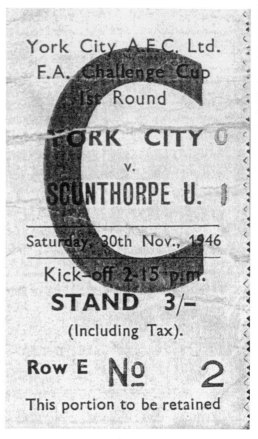

Above left and right: The programme and match ticket from Midland League Scunthorpe United's 1-0 victory over Third Division (North) York City at Bootham Crescent. A 4-1 defeat at Rotherham awaited them in the second round but after further success they were elected to the Football League in 1950.

Above: Ted Fenton (1914-1992) was born in Forest Gate. After a long career with West Ham, he was player-manager of Colchester at the time of their epic cup run of 1947/48 and later returned to manage the Hammers.

Opposite below: Southern League Colchester United were the sensations of the 1947/48 competition, reaching the fifth round before bowing out to the combined threat of the Stans-Matthews and Mortenson 5-0 at Blackpool. Before that, Banbury (2-1), and then Third Division (North) Wrexham (1-0), First Division Huddersfield (1-0) and Second Division Bradford PA (3-2) were all seen off at Layer Road. Pictured are both Colchester (in white shorts) and their First Division opponents Huddersfield lining up for posterity.

Above: Yeovil repeated the feat of Colchester the following season in beating a First Division team to reach the fifth round. Once again, a heavy defeat finally ended the run. The Glovers began their run quietly with victories over non-League Romford and Weymouth, both by emphatic 4-0 margins. Then came a 3-1 victory over Second Division Bury and a sensational 2-1 win over big-spending First Division Sunderland. The wheels finally came off in the next round with an 8-0 defeat to eventual winners Manchester United in front of 81,565 at Maine Road, as Old Trafford recovered from bomb damage sustained during the war.

Below: Yeovil goalkeeper Dyke clears from the striped Sunderland forwards at a packed Huish on 29 January 1949 in one of only six victories for non-League sides over First Division sides.

five

The 1950s

For the first time since the FA Cup was reorganised in 1925 a full decade of cup football was played. It provided the most successful set of results for non-Leaguers yet, with a tally of fifty-five Football League scalps being achieved by thirty clubs.

These excellent results looked far from likely at the start of the decade when four top non-League sides – Colchester United, Gillingham, Scunthorpe United and Shrewsbury Town – were elected to the Football League as it extended from the eighty-eight-member League it had been since 1921 to the new total of ninety-two. The loss of a quartet of the top sides was tempered by a tinkering with the first round of the cup that meant forty ties rather than thirty-six were now played, enabling non-League representation to increase from twenty-eight to thirty-two teams.

The 1950/51 season was a disaster with just one giantkilling – a victory for Ashington over Halifax which hardly registered on the Richter scale! Even worse, this was the only time not a single non-League team made the third round.

After this matters improved, driven by Peterborough United with eight giantkillings through the decade; Walthamstow and Bath also did well with four apiece and a trio of scalps were achieved by Bishop Auckland, Hereford and New Brighton.

Once again the Southern League achieved the best results with seventeen victories, closely followed by the Midland League (13) and Isthmian League (7), whilst the Northern League and Eastern Counties League made their first appearances. Peterborough got their just reward in 1960 and it would now be time for other sides to step into the spotlight and take some glory.

Giantkillers of the 1950s

(Non-League sides in capitals)

Season	Round					
1950/51	I	Halifax Town (FL3N)	2	ASHINGTON (NEL)	3	
1951/52	I	LEYTONSTONE (IL)	2	Shrewsbury Town (FL3S)	0	
	IR	Mansfield Town (FL3N)	0	STOCKTON (NEL)	2	
	2	BUXTON (CL)	4	Aldershot (FL3S)	3	
1952/53	I	BATH CITY (SL)	3	Southend United (FL3S)	1	
	I	PETERBOROUGH (ML)	2	Torquay United (FL3S)	1	
	2	FINCHLEY (AL)	3	Crystal Palace (FL3S)	1	
	2R	Watford (FL3S)	1	WALTHAMSTOW AVE (IL)	2	
	3R	WALTHAMSTOW AVE (IL)	2	Stockport County (FL3N)	1	
1953/54	I	GREAT YARMOUTH (ECL)	1	Crystal Palace (FL3S)	0	
	I	NUNEATON BOROUGH (BL)	3	Watford (FL3S)	0	
	I	WALTHAMSTOW AVE (IL)	1	Gillingham (FL3S)	0	
	IR	HEREFORD UNITED (SL)	2	Exeter City (FL3S)	0	
	IR	Newport County (FL3S)	1	CAMBRIDGE UTD (ECL)	2	
	IR	RHYL (CL)	4	Halifax Town (FL3N)	3	
	2	HASTINGS UNITED (SL)	4	Swindon Town (FL3S)	1	
	2	PETERBOROUGH UTD (ML)	2	Aldershot (FL3S)	1	
	2R	HEADINGTON (SL)	1	Millwall (FL3S)	0	
	3R	HEADINGTON (SL)	1	Stockport County (FL3N)	0	
1954/55	IR	WALTHAMSTOW AVE (IL)	4	Queens Park Rangers (FL3S)	0	
	2	Crystal Palace (FL3S)	2	BISHOP AUCKLAND (NL)	4	
	3R	BISHOP AUCKLAND (NL)	3	Ipswich Town (FL2)	0	
1955/56	I	PETERBOROUGH UTD (ML)	3	Ipswich Town (FL3S)	1	
	2	BEDFORD TOWN (SL)	3	Watford (FL3S)	2	
	2	Derby County (FL3N)	1	BOSTON UNITED (ML)	6	
	2R	BURTON ALBION (BL)	1	Halifax Town (FL3N)	0	
	2R	WORKSOP TOWN (ML)	1	Bradford City (FL3N)	0	
1956/57	I	BISHOP AUCKLAND (NL)	2	Tranmere Rovers (FL3N)	1	

	1	HEREFORD UTD (SL)	3	Aldershot (FL3S)	2
	1	Norwich City (FL3S)	2	BEDFORD TOWN (SL)	4
	1	WEYMOUTH (SL)	1	Shrewsbury Town (FL3S)	0
	1R	Stockport County (FL3N)	2	NEW BRIGHTON (CL)	3
	2	Derby County (FL3N)	2	NEW BRIGHTON (CL)	3
	2	PETERBOROUGH UTD (ML)	3	Bradford PA (FL3N)	0
	2R	Workington (FL3N)	0	GOOLE TOWN (ML)	1
	3	NEW BRIGHTON (CL)	2	Torquay United (FL3S)	1
	3	Notts County (FL2)	1	RHYL (CL)	3
	3R	Lincoln City (FL2)	4	PETERBOROUGH UTD (ML)	5
1957/58	1	BATH CITY (SL)	2	Exeter City (FL3S) 1	1
	1	Southport (FL3N)	1	WIGAN ATHLETIC (LC)	2
	1	WISBECH TOWN (ECL)	1	Colchester United (FL3S)	0
	2	HEREFORD UTD (SL)	6	Queens Park Rangers (FL3S)	1
1958/59	1	TOOTING (IL)	3	Bournemouth (FL3S)	1
	1R	YEOVIL TOWN (SL)	1	Southend United (FL3S)	0
	1R	SOUTH SHIELDS (ML)	5	Crewe (FL4)	0
	2	TOOTING (IL)	2	Northampton (FL3)	1
	2	WORCESTER CITY (SL)	5	Millwall (FL4)	2
	3	WORCESTER CITY (SL)	2	Liverpool (FL2)	1
1959/60	1	BATH CITY(SL)	3	Millwall (FL4)	1
	1	KING'S LYNN (SL)	3	Aldershot (FL4)	1
	1	PETERBOROUGH UTD (ML)	4	Shrewsbury Town (FL3)	3
	1	SOUTH SHIELDS (ML)	2	Chesterfield (FL3)	1
	2	Notts County (FL4)	0	BATH CITY (SL)	1
	2	Walsall (FL4)	2	PETERBOROUGH (ML)	3
	3	Ipswich Town (FL2)	2	PETERBOROUGH (ML)	3

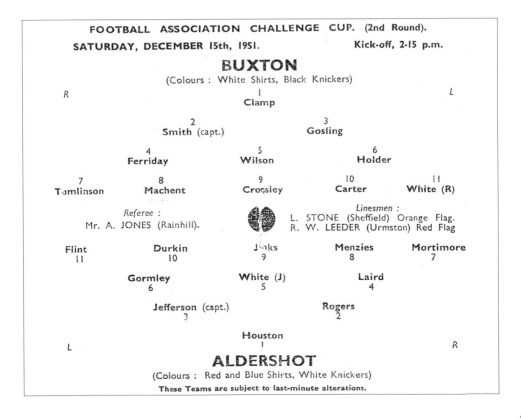

FOOTBALL ASSOCIATION CHALLENGE CUP. (2nd Round).

SATURDAY, DECEMBER 15th, 1951.   Kick-off, 2-15 p.m.

BUXTON
(Colours : White Shirts, Black Knickers)

R   1   L
Clamp

2
Smith (capt.)

3
Gosling

4
Ferriday

5
Wilson

6
Holder

7
Tomlinson

8
Machent

9
Crossley

10
Carter

11
White (R)

Referee :
Mr. A. JONES (Rainhill).

Linesmen :
L. STONE (Sheffield) Orange Flag.
R. W. LEEDER (Urmston) Red Flag

Flint
11

Durkin
10

Jacks
9

Menzies
8

Mortimore
7

Gormley
6

White (J)
5

Laird
4

Jefferson (capt.)
3

Rogers
2

Houston
1

L   R

ALDERSHOT
(Colours : Red and Blue Shirts, White Knickers)

These Teams are subject to last-minute alterations.

Previous and left: The programme and match report from the most dramatic day in the history of Buxton. Formed in 1877, Buxton had beaten Rawmarsh Welfare in the first round of the 1951/52 competition before achieving a dramatic 4-3 victory over Aldershot after leading 4-0 in just sixteen minutes. The third round saw them visit Second Division Doncaster Rovers, losing 2-0 after missing a penalty when 1-0 down.

Pros. outplayed by Leytonstone

Leytonstone 2, Shrewsbury 0

THIRD professional club to fall victims to the Leytonstone amateurs since the war, Shrewsbury Town might have fared much worse. Better balanced and using the ball more quickly and intelligently, Leytonstone had six or seven shots to every one of their opponents. Their fighting spirit was immense.

Mainstay of a hard-pressed Shrewsbury defence in a blank first half were centre half Depear, whose 6ft. plus towered over the home leader and harassed goalkeeper Egglestone, who had a severe testing time against the keen home forwards.

Leytonstone's richly deserved goals came in the first 12 minutes of the second half. Patrick and Groves had a hand in both. First, Patrick lifted a high centre which Joseph headed swiftly into the goalmouth for Groves to add the finishing touch. Then a splendid triangular move, initiated by Patrick, finished with Noble driving home a model centre by Groves for the second goal.

Leytonstone of the Isthmian League were worthy winners over Shrewsbury before losing out to Newport County in a second-round replay. The Isthmian Leaguers were founded in 1886 and merged with Ilford in 1989, later also merging with Redbridge Forest and then Dagenham & Redbridge in 1992.

Vic Groves

Vic Groves (1932–), born in Stepney, was one of three brothers to star in the Leytonstone side. After a spell with Leyton Orient, he returned to amateur football with Walthamstow Avenue. His fine forward play attracted Arsenal, who signed him in 1955, and he played nearly 200 games for them.

Len Julians

Len Julians (1933–1993). The Tottenham-born centre forward scored vital goals for Walthamstow Avenue before moving on to Leyton Orient, Arsenal and Nottingham Forest.

The fourth round paired Walthamstow Avenue with eventual champions Manchester United at Old Trafford, where a highly creditable 1-1 draw was achieved. Pictured is United's Allenby Chilton clashing with Avenue's best-known player, Jim Lewis, who was good enough to win a League Championship medal with Chelsea whilst remaining an amateur. Avenue lost the replay at Highbury 5-2 in front of 49,000. They beat five Football League clubs before merging in 1989 with Leytonstone-Ilford.

Above left: Walthstow Avenue were one of the great giantkilling teams of the 1950s. Their best season was 1952/53 when they beat Wimbledon and Watford and then overcame Stockport County 2-1. Pictured in stripes is Les Stratton preventing a threatening run from Stockport's grounded Jack Connor.

Above right: Finchley were founded in 1874 and had their best cup run in 1952/53. The Athenian Leaguers were beating Crystal Palace 3-1 when fog descended and the game was abandoned. Undaunted by this disappointment, they promptly repeated the dose four days later by the exact same scoreline. They had already beaten Kidderminster Harriers but went out in the third round 2-0 to Shrewsbury at Gay Meadow. The club eventually merged with Wingate to become Wingate & Finchley in 1992. Pictured is George Robb (1926-). The London-born left-winger was the star of the Finchley side that reached the third round in 1952/53. He went on to play for Tottenham and was one of the few post-war players to be capped for England at full and amateur levels

Jim Parks (1931-) was born in Haywards Heath and is better known as a cricketer, earning 46 caps for England as a wicketkeeper. His talent as a useful forward was underrated – he helped Hastings United to two successive trips to the third round of the FA Cup between 1953 and 1955.

Great Yarmouth narrowly failed to beat Wrexham in the 1952/53 season. A packed Wellesley Road watches the Bloaters goalkeeper Canning clear with the help of two defenders as they lost 2-1. The Norfolk side were formed in 1897 and are long time members of the Eastern Counties League. They had their best spell in the competition in the early 1950s and the highlight was the 1-0 victory over Crystal Palace in 1953/54 before losing 5-2 at Third Division North Barrow.

The joy of giantkilling can be seen as Headington fans carry Billy Smith off after his goal proved enough to beat Millwall 1–0 at the Manor Ground in a second-round replay on 17 December 1953.

The end of the dream for Headington as Ray Parry fires Bolton into a 2-0 lead in the fourth-round clash which they eventually won 4-2. The beaten goalkeeper is John Ansell, but Headington had already defeated Harwich, Millwall and Stockport in a dramatic run. Founded in 1893, they changed their name to Oxford United in 1960 and were Football League members between 1962 and 2006.

Opposite above left: Jack Fairbrother (1917-1999). The Burton-born goalkeeper won an FA Cup winners' medal with Newcastle in 1951. He later went on to manage Coventry and then Peterborough, for whom he helped establish a fearsome giantkilling reputation.

Opposite above right and below: The ever-improving Peterborough United were the non-League side to avoid in the 1950s. A string of Midland League titles and huge crowds enabled them to beat eight Football League clubs during the decade, and yet two fine sides were almostly completely different within just three years. The only common factor was outstanding centre half Norman Rigby. The club was formed in 1933 and elected to the Football League in 1960.

F.A. CHALLENGE CUP—3rd ROUND   JANUARY 9th, 1954

HALL   MATTHEWS   FAIRBROTHER   RIGBY   MOODY   ANDERSON

CAMPBELL   MARTIN   TAFT   SLOAN   HAIR

CARDIFF CITY v PETERBOROUGH UNITED

SHAW   DOUGLASS   RIGBY   WALLS   BARR   COCKBURN

HAILS   EMERY   DONALDSON   SMITH   HOGG

PETERBOROUGH UNITED F.C. 1956/57

Left: Henry Cockburn (1921-2004). The Ashton-born wing half enjoyed a long and fruitful career with Manchester United before moving on to Bury and then Peterborough, where he was a key member of the successful 1950s giantkilling team. He gained 13 international caps for England.

Below: Bishop Auckland were the kings of amateur football. Founded in 1886, the North Easterners were long-time members of the Northern League. They went on to win the Amateur Cup a record ten times and also recorded three victories over Football League sides in the FA Cup. The 1954/55 side reached the fourth round, beating Kettering, Crystal Palace and Ipswich before losing out to York.

Arsenal a blink from defeat

Arsenal .:.......................2   Bedford Town 2

ARSENAL Stadium's big clock showed less than 60 seconds to go. The floodlights blazed through mist in an electric atmosphere as Bedford, two goals down with 13 minutes to play but dramatically all square eight minutes later, surged forward.

The ball was flung out to right-winger Ronnie Steel. He slipped past Dennis Evans and raced for the end line.

Arsenal's defenders were at panic stations. Steel whipped across a powerful centre. Five yards from his own goal centre-half Jim Fotheringham stretched out a leg to prevent the pass reaching any of the four Bedford men up for the kill.

The ball flashed off his shin into the side net. As the net quivered everyone looked twice to see whether the ball was inside the Arsenal goal.

That is how near great fighters Bedford came to humiliating the club with the biggest name in British football.

For 77 minutes Bedford were outclassed. After goals by Derek Tapscott (12 minutes) and Vic Groves (50 minutes) Arsenal seemed anxious not to "rub it in." Chance after chance was wasted recklessly.

Suddenly Bedford pulled themselves together. Steel finished off an all-along-the-line attack to score with a rising shot Con Sullivan knew nothing about.

Ten thousand Bedford fans were in a frenzy. To a mounting roar, Felix Staroscik and Arthur Adey worked the ball along the left wing.

Adey centred and Sullivan reached for the ball, but Harry Yates's head delicately deflected it for Bernard Moore to ram in off the bar.

This greatest moment in Bedford's 47-year history was made possible by the magnificent play of centre-half Bob Craig and goalkeeper Terry Pope.

Cliff Holton starred for Arsenal in a match their supporters will never be allowed to forget.

Arsenal. — Sullivan; Charlton, Evans; Goring, Fotheringham, Holton; Clapton, Tapscott, Groves, Bloomfield, Tiddy.

Bedford Tn. — Pope; Cooke, Quinn; Farquhar, Craig, Garwood; Steel, Yates, Moore, Adey, Staroscik.

Above left: Bedford Town almost produced the greatest of all cup shocks in 1955/56 in two epic games with Arsenal. Having beaten Leyton and Norwich, the Southern Leaguers shook the Churners with tremendous performances at Highbury and then the Eyrie. This is the match report from the first game.

Above right: Jack Kelsey foils the eager Bedford forwards at an icy Eyrie in the replay.

Below left: The programme cover from the replay, watched by a record 15,000 crowd.

Below right: Felix Staroscik (1920–), the Polish-born winger who played a vital role in Bedford's great run of 1955/56.

Felix Staroscik

Weymouth have a good cup record and are seen here before the start of the 1955/56 campaign. Director Fred Meech appears to be giving a talk on tactics, while trainer Bill Hillier and secretary-manager Arthur Coles listen in. From left to right are: Pete McLean, Bill Hillier, Arthur Coles, Fred Meech, Bob McAlone, Sam McGowan, Jack Hobbs, Bill Thomas, Herny McGuinness, Willie Pagan and Jasper Youeil. The talk obviously worked as Weymouth beat Salisbury 3-2 before losing in the second round to Southend 1-0.

Reg Harrison

Boston United blitzed Derby County 6-1 on their own Baseball Ground in 1955/56 to equal the record victory for a non-League club over a Football League side. The humiliation was watched by 23,757 and one of six former Derby players now in the Pilgrims' colours was Reg Harrison (*above right*, 1923-), the Derby-born right-winger and member of the victorious Derby County cup-winning side of 1946. Having beaten Northwich as well as Derby they were paired away to Tottenham in the third round losing 4-0. Left back Geoff Snade heads off the line on this occasion.

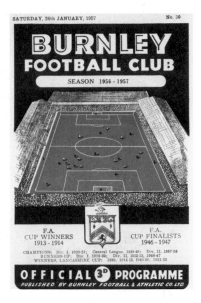

Above left: Albert Burgess (1919-1978). Born in Birkenhead, Burgess played for Bolton, Chester and York before helping New Brighton with a spectacular run in 1956/57. The inside forward helped New Brighton beat Stockport, Derby and Torquay before they were blitzed 9-0 by Burnley in the fourth round.

Above right and below left: The programme from that ill-fated mismatch. New Brighton were formed in 1921 and were Football League members between 1923 and 1951. The Rakers folded in 1983 after years of struggle.

Below right: Stan Hansen (1915-1987). Bootle born, Hansen was a long-serving goalkeeper with Bolton. He helped Rhyl reach the fourth round of the FA Cup in 1956/57 with a string of fine performances as the Cheshire Leaguers beat Scarborough, Bishop Auckland and Notts County before losing 3-0 at Bristol City.

Above left: Warren Bradley (1933-2007). The Hyde-born winger scored the winner for Bishop Auckland against Tranmere in the 1956/57 competition and moved to Manchester United in 1958, achieving three England caps to go with a string of amateur caps.

Above right: Jesse Pye (1919-1984). Born in Treeton, Pye – a centre forward capped by England – had a long career with Wolves. In the twilight of his career, he scored the goal that saw Wisbech tip Colchester out of the 1957/58 competition. The Fenmen, formed in 1920, still await another giantkilling.

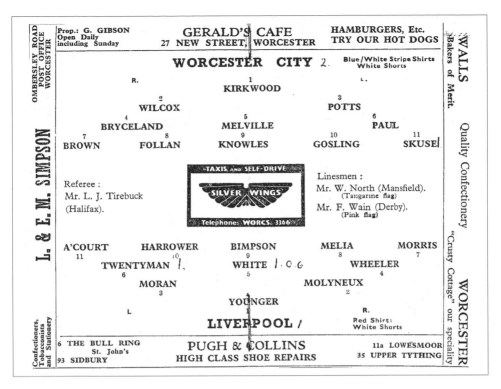

WORCESTER CITY 2.

Blue/White Stripe Shirts
White Shorts

R.   **1**   L.
KIRKWOOD

2   **WILCOX**   **3**   **POTTS**

4   **BRYCELAND**   **5**   **MELVILLE**   **6**   **PAUL**

7   **BROWN**   **8**   **FOLLAN**   **9**   **KNOWLES**   **10**   **GOSLING**   **11**   **SKUSE**

Referee :
Mr. L. J. Tirebuck
(Halifax).

Linesmen :
Mr. W. North (Mansfield).
(Tangarine flag)
Mr. F. Wain (Derby).
(Pink flag)

11   **A'COURT**   **HARROWER**   **9**   **BIMPSON**   **8**   **MELIA**   **7**   **MORRIS**

10   **TWENTYMAN**   **5**   **WHITE 1. O.G**   **4**   **WHEELER**

6   **MORAN**   **2**   **MOLYNEUX**
3

YOUNGER
1
L   R.

LIVERPOOL 1

Red Shirt;
White Shorts

Above: The line-up for the Worcester City *v.* Liverpool game of 1959. Worcester were formed in 1902 and currently play in the Conference North.

Below: Teenager Tommy Skuse beats Dick White to put Worcester ahead as Liverpool's Scottish international goalkeeper Tommy Younger can only look on.

Opposite, below left: Roy Paul (1920-2002). The Ton Pentre-born Welsh international wing half skippered Manchester City to 1956 FA Cup triumph. He then captained Worcester in the sensational run of 1958/59 that saw them beat Chelmsford, Millwall and Liverpool before bowing out to Sheffield United in front of a massive St George's Lane crowd of 17,042.

Opposite, below right: The match programme before the bad weather caused a five-day delay.

Above: The Tooting Terrors who shared top billing with Worcester in 1958/59. The line-up was, from left to right, back row: Viney, Edwards, Grainger, Pearson, Murphy, Bennett, Slade. Front row: Holden, Harlow, Hasty, Flanagan. The club was formed in 1931 through the amalgamation of Tooting (founded in 1887) and Mitcham (1912). Then, as now, Tooting were members of the Isthmian League.

Below left: The second round saw Tooting beat Northampton 2-1, as shown in this cartoon.

Below right: Charlie Fleming (1927-1997). The Scottish forward, nicknamed 'Cannonball' for his powerful shooting, played for East Fife and Sunderland before a long stay with Bath that featured several cup runs.

Above left: Tony Book (1934-). Bath born, it was at his home-town club that he made his mark as an influential full-back, helping the side to the third round of the FA Cup in 1959/60. He later moved to Plymouth and then Manchester City, gaining League and cup success.

Above right: Malcolm Allison (1927-). Dartford-born 'Big Mal' was a larger-than-life character who came into his own as a coach after playing centre half for West Ham. He was at Bath when the cup run of 1959/60 set him on his way, and he moved on to Plymouth and then Manchester City, collecting plenty of silverware in the process.

Below left and right: The Bath versus Brighton programme.

Peterborough United collected three more Football League scalps in 1959/60 in what proved to be their final season as a non-League side. A thrilling 4-3 victory over Shrewsbury was followed by a 3-2 victory at Walsall, and then came another 3-2 win at Ipswich. Pictured is Posh full-back Jim Walker trying to stop Aled Owen from crossing as the snow falls. Sheffield Wednesday finally ended their run with a 2-0 victory. At the AGM of the Football League in May 1960 they were elected to replace Gateshead after years of trying.

six

The 1960s

The 1960s failed to live up to the success of the 1950s with just forty-two giantkillings against the fifty-five of the previous decade (it was now possible to draw comparisons as a second full decade was completed).

Bedford Town were the top club of the decade, not only beating four Football League clubs but twice almost beating mighty Arsenal. Yeovil built on their reputation, taking three scalps – the same as South Shields. The victories were spread around, with thirty-one clubs securing the forty-two wins.

Once again the Southern League – now extended from twenty-two to forty-four clubs – were the most dominant, claiming twenty-six of the victims. The Cheshire League picked up five victories but the once powerful Midland League were in a serious decline with just one victory – the same as the Northern Premier League, formed late in the decade but soon to be a powerful force.

For the first time ever there were all-non-League clashes in the third round as Weymouth beat Morecambe 1-0 in 1961/62, Bedford beat Hereford 2-1 in 1965/66 and Sutton beat Hillingdon 4-1 in a replay. For all of the clubs, but particularly the losers, this was the height of frustration – to get so far only to meet fellow non-Leaguers!

Giantkillers of the 1960s

(Non-League sides in capitals)

1960/61	1	BANGOR CITY (CL)		1	Wrexham (FL4)		0
	1	Walsall (FL3)		0	YEOVIL (SL)		1
1961/62	1	Bournemouth (FL3)		0	MARGATE (SL)		3
	1	Tranmere Rovers (FL4)		2	GATESHEAD (NCL)		3
	1R	DARTFORD (SL)		2	Exeter City (FL4)		1
	1R	KETTERING (SL)		3	Swindon (FL3)		0
	2	Chester City (FL4)		0	MORECAMBE (LC)		1
	2	Coventry (FL3)		1	KING'S LYNN (SL)		2
	2	WEYMOUTH (SL)		1	Newport County (FL3)		0
1962/63	1	GRAVESEND (SL)		3	Exeter City (FL4)		2
	1	WIMBLEDON (IL)		2	Colchester United (FL3)		1
	3	Carlisle (FL3)		0	GRAVESEND (SL)		1
1963/64	1	Darlington (FL4)		1	GATESHEAD (NRL)		4
	1	YEOVIL (SL)		1	Southend (FL3)		0
	1R	Millwall (FL3)		2	KETTERING (SL)		3
	2	YEOVIL (SL)		3	Crystal Palace (FL3)		1
	3	Newcastle (FL2)		1	BEDFORD (SL)		2
1964/65	1	CROOK TOWN (NL)		1	Carlisle (FL3)		0
	1	SCARBOROUGH (ML)		1	Bradford City (FL4)		0
	1R	SOUTH LIVERPOOL (LC)		4	Halifax (FL4)		2
1965/66	1	BATH CITY (SL)		2	Newport County (FL4)		0
	1	Exeter City (FL3)		1	BEDFORD (SL)		2
	1	Gillingham (FL3)		1	FOLKESTONE (SL)		2
	1	SOUTH SHIELDS (NRL)		3	York City (FL3)		1
	1R	WIGAN (CL)		3	Doncaster Rovers (FL4)		1
	2	HEREFORD (SL)		1	Millwall (FL3)		0
	2	Rochdale (FL4)		1	ALTRINCHAM (CL)		3
	2R	BEDFORD (SL)		2	Brighton (FL3)		1
	2R	Luton Town (FL4)		0	CORBY TOWN (SL)		1
1966/67	2	NUNEATON (SL)		2	Swansea (FL3)		0
	2R	BEDFORD (SL)		1	Oxford United (FL3)		0
1967/68	1	RUNCORN (CL)		1	Notts County (FL4)		0
	1	TOW LAW TOWN (NL)		5	Mansfield Town (FL3)		1
	1R	GUILDFORD CITY (SL)		2	Brentford (FL4)		1
	1R	MACCLESFIELD (CL)		2	Stockport (FL3)		1

	1R	CHELMSFORD (SL)	1	Oxford United (FL3)	0
1968/69	1	DARTFORD (SL)	3	Aldershot (FL4)	1
1969/70	1	BRENTWOOD (SL)	1	Reading (FL3)	0
	1	SOUTH SHIELDS (NPL)	2	Bradford PA (FL4)	1
	1	TAMWORTH (WMRL)	2	Torquay United (FL3)	1
	2	HILLINGDON BORO (SL)	2	Luton Town (FL3)	1
	2R	Oldham (FL4)	1	SOUTH SHIELDS (NPL)	2

Deserved Win for King's Lynn

COVENTRY CITY 1, KING'S LYNN 2

NOVEMBER 25, 1961—this is the day that Coventry City followers will long remember as Black Saturday. In probably the most grim page in City's modern history, a team of part-timers from King's Lynn inscribed their indelible mark by sweeping their Third Division opponents out of the F.A. Cup, leaving shocked and stunned City fans to wonder how a League side could have offered such puny and deplorably inept resistance.

Shock results have happened before. In fact, since Walsall did their famous giant-killing act on Arsenal all those years ago, they have become almost commonplace.

But City's answer in their own, familiar Highfield Road surroundings. to the eager, thrusting play of the bricklayers and clerks of King's Lynn was so slipshod, it had to be witnessed to be believed.

No doubt the 11,000 or so City fans in the 12,080 crowd will want to forget as quickly as possible—but does one easily forget a nightmare?

Wrong Approach

One is ready for shocks at any stage of the Cup. And in admitting I and many others were hopelessly wrong in thinking Lynn could not come to Coventry and conquer, I offer them my hearty congratulations for a plucky and often skilful display.

City's strolling attitude to this whole tie was not just dangerously complacent, it was sheer folly.

In practically every phase of the game, including staying power, City played second fiddle. They passed atrociously, shot wildly,

By NEMO

slowed their game down to a pace when it was child's play for them to be tackled and robbed with astonishing frequency, and, worst of all, they failed to supply the second-half rally expected of them.

Picture the shocked scene at Highfield Road. City had been literally given a goal after 28 minutes when centre-half Hindle, trying to boot the ball away for a corner, unluckily sliced it against goalkeeper Manning and it flew into the net.

One would have expected this to knock out the heart from the Linnets and encourage the City to shake themselves from their lethargy. But it had the opposite effect.

Last-minute substitute Mick Johnson, deputising for flu-victim Bobby Brennan, snapped up a Wright pass to hit a left-foot shot past Lightening in the 33rd minute, then, lo and behold, Lynn took the lead three minutes later when Wright sent a cracking header over the line off the City crossbar.

Chance Squandered

These goals were the result of snappy through-passing which City never seem to be able to accomplish themselves these days, plus slack marking and, I thought, a little slowness on Lightening's part in making an attempt to stop both goals.

The number of times Imlach an Peter Hill were tackled and robbed was legion, and inside them, Dixon and Hewitt were snuffed out so effectively that the Lynn forwards needed only those two snap efforts to buy a ticket into the next round.

"Wait until the second half—the pace will tell on King's Lynn," was the optimistic forecast from some when City trailed in 2-1 down at the interval.

But, sad to tell, it was City who flagged and after seeming to falter just for a moment or two, the part-timers came back to finish strong winners.

King's Lynn had a great run in 1961/62. They surprised Southern League champions Chelmsford with a 2-1 win and then again on their travels beat Third Division Coventry City by the same score. A lucrative third-round tie at eventual First Division champions Everton ended in a 4-0 defeat. The club – formed in 1879 – still await another giantkilling.

Dartford overcame Exeter 2-1 after a battling 3-3 draw in Devon. Sadly, they were crushed by Bristol City in the next round.

Alf Ackerman (1929-1988). The South African-born centre forward scored plenty of goals in the lower divisions before joining Dartford as player-manager and helping them to knock Exeter off the Wembley trail – their first giantkilling for twenty-five years.

After the reorganisation of the cup in 1925, the tally of successful non-League giantkillers had reached 145 by 2007. Romford have tried harder than most to join that club, so far without success. Pictured are the squad in training for another unsuccessful joust with Football League opposition – this time Watford in 1961/62, who won 3-1. Romford player-manager Ted Ditchburn – the former Tottenham and England goalkeeper – leads the way on this training session.

Above left: John Roche (1932–1988). Born in Poplar, the inside forward was a key member of the Margate side in 1961/62, scoring the opening goal in a stunning 3-0 win over Third Division leaders Bournemouth. They lost to Notts County 2-0 in a second-round replay.

Above right: Jack Froggatt (1922–1993). The Sheffield-born centre half had an outstanding career with Portsmouth and Leicester before moving to Kettering, where his experience was vital in their fine 3-0 demolition of Swindon in 1961/62. The team lost to local rivals Northampton 3-0 in the next round.

Opposite: History was made on 6 January 1962 when two non-League sides clashed in the third round of the FA Cup. The sides meeting – Morecambe and Weymouth – must have had mixed feelings. It was for both probably their best chance of reaching the fourth round, but their original dreams of meeting a top side had to go on the back burner. The Lancashire Combination side had beaten South Shields and Fourth Division Chester, whilst the Southern Leaguers had overcome Barnet and Third Division Newport County. When the dust settled at Christie Park that day, the Dorset visitors won through by a single goal, scored by Ron Fogg and watched by a 9,383 crowd. The Terras lost 2-0 at Preston in the fourth round.

MORECAMBE F.C.

3ʳᵈ ROUND F.A.CUP

MORECAMBE

V

WEYMOUTH

christie park ·· jan 6 1962.

souvenir programme

Previous and above: The 1961/62 Morecambe team met Weymouth in the third round. It was the first ever occasion two non-Leaguers had met at this stage.

The Weymouth side of 1961/62.

Wimbledon produced their first giantkilling in 1962/63 with a 2-1 win over Third Division Colchester. This was their best season since their formation in 1889 as they also won the FA Amateur Cup for the only time. An astonishing climb up the footballing ladder saw them rise from Southern League champions (1977) to FA Cup winners (1988) in just eleven years.

Johnny Crossan (second right) makes it 4-0 to Sunderland at a frozen Roker Park. Bob McNicol, the Gravesend captain (far right), still had time to score and get sent off in the 5-2 defeat.

Harry McDonald (1926-2004). Born in Ashton, McDonald was a fine full-back for Crystal Palace and Gravesend, and saw both sides of the cup. With Palace he suffered three successive giantkillings in the 1950s at the hands of Finchley, Great Yarmouth and Bishop Auckland, but he saw success with Gravesend in their long run in 1962/63.

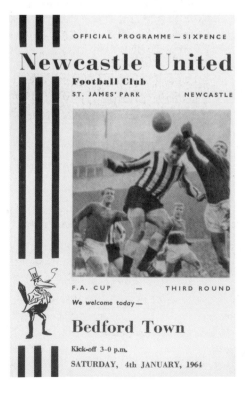

Bedford Town continued their series of giantkillings with a shock 2-1 win at Newcastle. It was their third and best of six victories over Football League sides. The fourth round saw them lose 3-0 to Carlisle. The club was formed in 1908 and folded in 1981 before reforming in 1989.

Jock Wallace

Right: John 'Jock' Wallace (1935-1996) – born in Wallyford – started as goalkeeper with Airdrie and later West Brom before moving to Bedford as player-manager, inspiring them to some great cup exploits. He later managed Leicester and Glasgow Rangers.

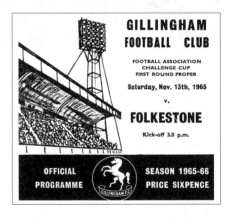

GILLINGHAM FOOTBALL CLUB

FOOTBALL ASSOCIATION
CHALLENGE CUP
FIRST ROUND PROPER

Saturday, Nov. 13th, 1965

v.

FOLKESTONE

Kick-off 3.0 p.m.

OFFICIAL PROGRAMME

SEASON 1965-66 PRICE SIXPENCE

Right and below: Folkestone upset the odds in the Kentish derby by beating Third Division Gillingham in their own Priestfield backyard. After winning at Wimbledon in the second round, they were beaten 5-1 at home by Crewe in the third round – a disappointing end to a fine cup run.

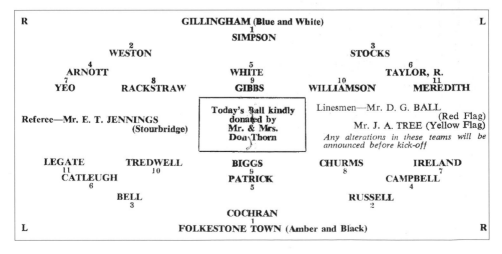

R   **GILLINGHAM** (Blue and White)   L
1
SIMPSON

2   3
WESTON   **STOCKS**

4   5   6
ARNOTT   **WHITE**   **TAYLOR, R.**
7   8   9   10   11
YEO   **RACKSTRAW**   **GIBBS**   **WILLIAMSON**   **MEREDITH**

Referee—Mr. E. T. JENNINGS   Today's Ball kindly   Linesmen—Mr. D. G. BALL
                (Stourbridge)   donated by   (Red Flag)
                                       Mr. & Mrs.   Mr. J. A. TREE (Yellow Flag)
                                       Don Thorn   *Any alterations in these teams will be
                                                            announced before kick-off*

LEGATE   **TREDWELL**   **BIGGS**   **CHURMS**   **IRELAND**
11   10   9   8   7
CATLEUGH   **PATRICK**   **CAMPBELL**
6   5   4
       BELL   **RUSSELL**
       3   2
                                     COCHRAN
                                          1
L   **FOLKESTONE TOWN** (Amber and Black)   R

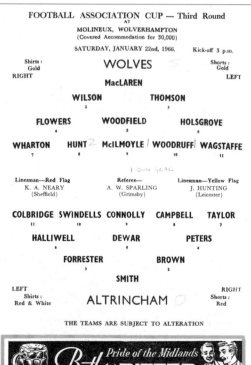

FOOTBALL ASSOCIATION CUP — Third Round
AT
MOLINEUX, WOLVERHAMPTON
(Covered Accommodation for 30,000)

SATURDAY, JANUARY 22nd, 1966.   Kick-off 3 p.m.

Shirts :   Shorts :
Gold   **WOLVES**   Gold
RIGHT   LEFT

MacLAREN

WILSON   THOMSON
2   3

FLOWERS   WOODFIELD   HOLSGROVE
4   5   6

WHARTON   HUNT   McILMOYLE WOODRUFF WAGSTAFFE
7   8   9   10   11

Linesman—Red Flag   Referee—   Linesman—Yellow Flag
K. A. NEARY   A. W. SPARLING   J. HUNTING
(Sheffield)   (Grimsby)   (Leicester)

COLBRIDGE SWINDELLS CONNOLLY CAMPBELL TAYLOR
11   10   9   8   7

HALLIWELL   DEWAR   PETERS
6   5   4

FORRESTER   BROWN
3   2

SMITH

LEFT   RIGHT
Shirts :   Shorts :
Red & White   **ALTRINCHAM**   Red

THE TEAMS ARE SUBJECT TO ALTERATION

Above and left: Freddie Pye (1928-). Born in Stockport, Pye was an inside forward with Accrington and Stalybridge but was better known for putting Altrincham on the map with a fine run in the 1965/66 season – this was the start of a successful two decades for the club. They crushed Scarborough 6-0 in the first round, then went to Spotland and beat Fourth Division Rochdale 3-1, before coming up against Wolves and suffering a 5-0 defeat at Molineaux.

NUNEATON BOROUGH
Football Club Limited

2nd.
ROUND
FOOTBALL
ASSOCIATION
CUP

NUNEATON BOROUGH
v
SWANSEA TOWN

SATURDAY
JANUARY
7th.
1967

KICK OFF
3
p.m.

OFFICIAL PROGRAMME 1/-

NUNEATON BOROUGH
Football Club Limited

3rd.
ROUND
FOOTBALL
ASSOCIATION
CUP

NUNEATON BOROUGH
v
ROTHERHAM UTD.

SATURDAY
JANUARY
28th.
1967

KICK OFF
3
p.m.

OFFICIAL PROGRAMME 1/-

Above left and right: Nuneaton Borough had their best run in 1966/67, reaching the third round for the first time with victories over Wealdstone and more notably Swansea 2-0. Two tight games against Rotherham eventually saw a narrow 1-0 replay defeat after a 1-1 draw at Manor Park in front of a 22,114 crowd.

Right: John Watts (1931-). Born in Birmingham, Watts had a long career with his home-town club before moving to Nuneaton, where he featured strongly in their outstanding run of 1966/67.

John Watts

Sid Bishop

Above left: Sid Bishop (1934-). The Tooting-born Leyton Orient stalwart ended his career with Guildford, helping them to a memorable victory over Brentford in 1967/68 in his centre-half role.

Above right: Tow Law Town crushed Mansfield 5-1 to record their only cup slaying. They gave Shrewsbury a torrid time in the second round too, but were held 1-1 and suffered a 6-2 replay defeat. The next season Mansfield were drawn at home to the Lawyers and took revenge 4-1. The club were formed in 1890 and are still members of the Northern League.

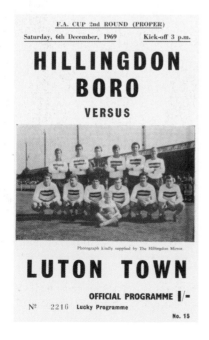

Jim Langley

Opposite, below left: Hillingdon Borough surprised Third Division Luton Town by beating them 2-1 in the second round of the 1969/70 competition, having beaten Wimbledon in the opening round. Their luck ran out in the third round when they faced fellow non-Leaguers Sutton United, losing 4-1 in a replay. Their fortunes deteriorated in the 1980s and the club folded in 1985.

Opposite, below right: Jim Langley (1929-). Born in Kilburn, the stylish former Brighton, Fulham and QPR full-back proved an excellent player-manager for Hillingdon, belying his forty years.

Right: Pat Terry (1933-). Born in Lambeth, Terry was another well-travelled player who always ensured defenders had their hands full in his centre forward role. He joined Hillingdon in time to play a key role in their 1969/70 cup run to the third round.

Pat Terry

Steve Gammon

John Ritchie

Above left: Steve Gammon (1939-), the Swansea-born wing half who was desperately unlucky with injuries – three broken legs seriously damaging his career. He moved into the role of player-manager, helping Kettering to plenty of cup success in the mid-1960s.

Above right: John Ritchie (1941-). The Kettering-born centre forward made his name with his home-town club, netting in the 3-0 triumph over Swindon in 1961/62 before being snapped up by Stoke.

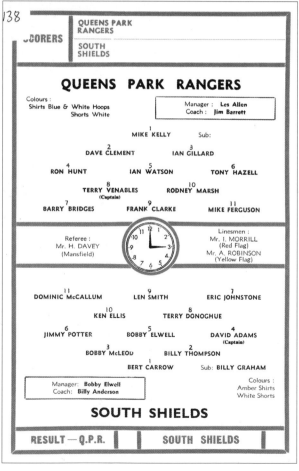

Above: South Shields had their best run since their formation in 1936 in the competition of 1969/70, beating two Fourth Division sides in the opening two rounds. Bradford PA and Oldham were both defeated 2-1 – the Latics after a 0-0 draw – before QPR proved too strong by a 4-1 margin. The club folded in 1974.

Left: The programme from the QPR versus South Shields game.

seven

The 1970s

The 1970s provided great success with a record 75 victories for non-Leaguers against Football League opposition. Three of the more successful clubs were even able to break into the Football League despite the presence at the time of the notorious 'Old Pals Act' which protected their weaker League clubs long after natural justice had told them it was time to go.

In the end, sheer ability on and off the pitch were vital but the icing on the cake for each of the clubs was a thrilling FA Cup run, and so Hereford (1972), Wimbledon (1977) and Wigan (1978) took their place in the Football League with the latter two at various stages going all the way to the top division.

The best run in a vintage decade came from Blyth Spartans in 1977/78 when they emulated Colchester and Yeovil thirty years earlier in reaching the fifth round. They also made up a fourth all-non-League clash in the third round when they beat Enfield 1-0 – all four clashes came in the period between 1961/62 and 1977/78, and no more have occurred before or since. The success of Blyth helped to achieve a record 12 victories for non-League sides over Football League clubs that season – beating the 1956/57 record of 11 – and the record would last until 2000/01, when 13 victories would be achieved.

Wigan and Scarborough with five wins apiece and Blyth, Leatherhead and Altrincham with four led the way among the clubs, whilst the Northern Premier League usurped the Southern League as the top giantkilling league with 26 victories against 19. The Isthmian had their best tally with 16 whilst the newly formed Alliance Premier League had a disappointing start with just two wins.

Giantkillers of the 1970s

(Non-League sides in capitals)

Season	Round	Team	Goals	Opponent	Goals
1970/71	1	BARNET (SL)	6	Newport County (FL4)	1
	1	GRANTHAM (ML)	2	Stockport County (FL4)	1
	1	RHYL (CC)	1	Hartlepool United (FL4)	0
	1	Southport (FL4)	0	BOSTON UNITED (NPL)	2
	1R	Northampton (FL4)	1	HEREFORD UNITED (SL)	2
	2	Bournemouth (FL4)	0	YEOVIL (SL)	1
	2	WIGAN ATHLETIC (NPL)	2	Peterborough (FL4)	1
	2R	RHYL (CC)	2	Barnsley (FL4)	0
1971/72	1	Crewe (FL4)	0	BLYTH SPARTANS (NL)	1
	1	WIGAN ATHLETIC (NPL)	2	Halifax (FL3)	1
	1R	Scunthorpe Utd (FL4)	2	SOUTH SHIELDS (NPL)	3
	2	BLYTH SPARTANS (NL)	1	Stockport County (FL4)	0
	2	BOSTON UNITED (NPL)	1	Hartlepool Utd (FL4)	1
	2R	HEREFORD UTD (SL)	2	Northampton (FL4)	1
	3R	HEREFORD UTD (SL)	2	Newcastle Utd (FL1)	1
1972/73	1	HAYES (IL)	1	Bristol Rovers (FL3)	0
	1	MARGATE (SL)	1	Swansea (FL3)	0
	1	Rochdale (FL3)	1	BANGOR CITY (NPL)	2
	1	WALTON (IL)	2	Exeter City (FL4)	1
	1	YEOVIL (SL)	2	Brentford (FL3)	1
	1R	SCARBOROUGH (NPL)	2	Oldham (FL3)	1
1973/74	1	ALTRINCHAM (NPL)	2	Hartlepool Utd (FL4)	0
	1	Exeter City (FL4)	0	ALVECHURCH (WMRL)	1
	1	WYCOMBE (IL)	3	Newport (FL4)	1
	1R	Brighton(FL3)	0	WALTON (IL)	4
	1R	SCARBOROUGH (NPL)	2	Crewe (FL4)	1
	2R	Rochdale (FL3)	3	GRANTHAM (SL)	5
1974/75	1R	ALTRINCHAM (NPL)	3	Scunthorpe(FL4)	1
	1R	GATESHEAD (NPL)	1	Crewe (FL4)	0
	1R	KETTERING (SL)	3	Swansea (FL4)	1

	1R	STAFFORD RANGERS (NPL)	1	Stockport (FL4)	0
	1R	WIGAN ATHLETIC (NPL)	2	Shrewsbury (FL4)	1
	2	LEATHERHEAD (IL)	1	Colchester (FL3)	0
	2	STAFFORD RANGERS (NPL)	2	Halifax (FL3)	1
	2R	Bournemouth (FL3)	1	WYCOMBE (IL)	2
	3	Brighton (FL3)	0	LEATHERHEAD (IL)	1
	3	Burnley (FL1)	0	WIMBLEDON (SL)	1
	3R	Rotherham (FL4)	0	STAFFORD RANGERS (NPL)	2
1975/76	1	COVENTRY SPORTING (WMRL)	2	Tranmere Rovers (FL4)	0
	1	Grimsby (FL3)	1	GATESHEAD (NPL)	3
	1	HENDON (IL)	1	Reading (FL4)	0
	1	LEATHERHEAD (IL)	2	Cambridge United (FL3)	0
	1	MARINE (CC)	3	Barnsley (FL4)	1
	1	SPENNYMOOR (NL)	4	Southport (FL4)	1
	1R	DOVER (SL)	4	Colchester (FL3)	1
	2	SCARBOROUGIH (NPL)	3	Preston (FL3)	2
	3R	TOOTING (IL)	2	Swindon (FL3)	1
1976/77	1	LEATHERHEAD (IL)	2	Northampton (FL4)	0
	1	Swansea (FL4)	0	MINEHEAD (SL)	1
	1	Torquay (FL4)	1	HILLINGDON BOROUGH (SL)	2
	1R	Oxford United (FL3)	0	KETTERING (SL)	1
	1R	NORTHWICH VICTORIA (NPL)	2	Rochdale (FL4)	1
	2	Mansfield Town (FL3)	2	MATLOCK TOWN (NPL)	5
	2	NORTHWICH VICTORIA (NPL)	4	Peterborough Utd (FL3)	0
	3	NORTHWICH VICTORIA (NPL)	3	Watford (FL4)	2
1977/78	1	ENFIELD (IL)	3	Wimbledon (FL4)	0
	1	NUNEATON (SL)	2	Oxford United (FL3)	0
	1	SCARBOROUGH (NPL)	4	Rochdale (FL4)	2
	1	WIGAN ATHLETIC (NPL)	1	York City (FL4)	3
	1R	Hereford United (FL3)	2	WEALDSTONE (SL)	3
	1R	RUNCORN (NPL)	1	Southport (FL4)	0
	2	BLYTH SPARTANS (NL)	1	Chesterfield (FL3)	0
	2	Northampton (FL4)	0	ENFIELD (IL)	2
	2	WEALDSTONE (SL)	2	Reading (FL4)	1
	2	WIGAN ATHLETIC (NPL)	1	Sheffield Wednesday (FL3)	0
	2R	SCARBOROUGH (NPL)	2	Crewe (FL4)	0
	4	Stoke City (FL2)	2	BLYTH SPARTANS (NL)	3
1978/79	1	Rochdale (FL4)	0	DROYLESDON (CC)	1
	1	WORCESTER CITY (SL)	2	Plymouth Argyle (FL3)	0
	2	MAIDSTONE UTD (SL)	1	Exeter City (FL3)	0
1979/80	1	ALTRINCHAM (APL)	3	Crewe (FL4)	0
	1	BARKING (IL)	1	Oxford United (FL3)	0
	2	Rotherham Utd (FL3)	0	ALTRINCHAM (APL)	2
	2R	HARLOW (IL)	1	Southend United (FL3)	0
	3R	HARLOW (IL)	1	Leicester City (FL2)	0

Southern League Barnet scorched to a 6–1 win over Newport County in the first round of the 1970/71 competition, equalling the record victory achieved by Wigan against Carlisle in 1934/35, Walthamstow versus Northampton in 1936/37, Boston United versus Derby in 1955/56 and Hereford against QPR in 1957/58. Ricky George (second left) starts the slaughter with the first goal – he was to score the winner for Hereford against Newcastle the following season.

Colin Powell fires in the fourth goal.

Cambridge United were one of the few clubs to gain election to the Football League without a cup giantkilling history. They were founded as Abbey United in 1919 and changed to their present name in 1951. Their only victims were Newport County in 1953/54 but two successive Southern League titles won them their Football League place in 1970, and in their first cup game as League members they faced a tricky tie at Enfield, just getting home by 1–0. George Harris of Cambridge is sandwiched by Tony Gibson and Ken Gray.

Above and below left: The tremendous cup run of Hereford United is what legends are made of.

Below right: Bournemouth had to wait eleven years for revenge over Margate following their 1960/61 3-0 defeat. This time around, with Ted MacDougall (pictured) scoring nine goals, there was no hiding place as the Southern Leaguers crumbled to an 11-0 defeat.

Opposite above: The Margate side pictured earlier in the 1971/72 season before the fateful trip to Dean Court.

Right: Rhyl had their last decent cup run as long ago as 1970/71 with a trip to the third round and a 6-1 defeat against their fellow Welshmen Swansea. They had beaten Barnsley and Hartlepool on the way, chalking up seven giantkillings. Formed in 1870 as Rhyl Skull & Crossbones, they now play in the Welsh League and no longer enter the competition.

The biggest day in the proud FA Cup history of Margate came in 1972/73 when they entertained Tottenham at Hartsdown Park before a record 8,500 crowd for their third-round tussle. They had already beaten Walton and Swansea but found Spurs a different proposition, losing 6-0. Martin Chivers is about to open the scoring from a free-kick.

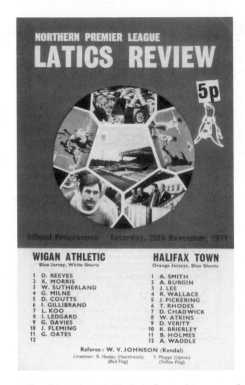

NORTHERN PREMIER LEAGUE
LATICS REVIEW

5p

Official Programme   Saturday, 20th November, 1971

WIGAN ATHLETIC	HALIFAX TOWN
Blue Jersey, White Shorts	Orange Jerseys, Blue Shorts
1 D. REEVES	1 A. SMITH
2 K. MORRIS	2 A. BURGIN
3 W. SUTHERLAND	3 J. LEE
4 G. MILNE	4 R. WALLACE
5 D. COUTTS	5 J. PICKERING
6 I. GILLIBRAND	6 T. RHODES
7 L. KOO	7 D. CHADWICK
8 I. LEDGARD	8 W. ATKINS
9 G. DAVIES	9 D. VERITY
10 J. FLEMING	10 K. BRIERLEY
11 G. OATES	11 B. HOLMES
12	12 A. WADDLE

Referee: W. V. JOHNSON (Kendal)
Linesmen: B. Healey (Northwich)   F. Phipps (Upton)
(Red Flag)   (Yellow Flag)

Howard Wilkinson

Above left: Wigan Athletic – formed in 1932 after the demise of Football League side Wigan Borough – chalked up their sixth Football League conquest with a 2-1 victory over Third Division Halifax Town in 1971.

Above right and below: Boston United reached the third round for a third time in 1971/72, having beaten Ellesmere Port and Hartlepool United in the opening two rounds. Two distinguished future managers, Jim Smith and Howard Wilkinson, featured in the Pilgrims side but the Northern Premier Leaguers lost out to Second Division Portsmouth by 1-0 before a near-11,000 York Street crowd.

Isthmian Leaguers Hayes created a
shock with a 1-0 win over Bristol
Rovers on 18 November 1972
courtesy of a Bobby Hatt goal, and a
single-goal replay victory for Reading
ended their run in the second round.
Terry Brown (front row, third left)
later took them into the Conference
as manager and also repeated the trick
with Aldershot.

Walton & Hersham were formed in
1945 and made a big impact in the
seventies, beating Exeter and then
more spectacularly Brighton 4-0 at
the Goldstone with a hat-trick from
Clive Foskett. A trip to Edgar Street
saw them lose 3-0 to Hereford in the
second round.

Scarborough were a constant scourge to Football League clubs through the years and the 1972/73
vintage were no exception. A replay victory saw them beat Oldham – their fifth Football League victims.
Doncaster Rovers ended their run at Seamer Road 2-1 in the second round. They were elected to
the Football League in 1987 losing their place in 1999. A stunning cup run in 2003/04 saw them face
Chelsea in the fourth round losing narrowly 1-0. After this it was all downhill for the Seadogs eventually
after successive relegations they went into liquidation in 2007. Their nine giantkillings make them sixth
in the all time list.

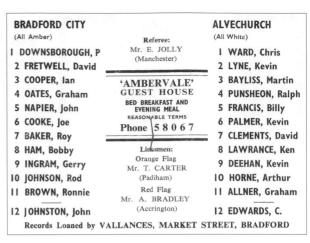

BRADFORD CITY		ALVECHURCH
(All Amber)	Referee:	(All White)
1 DOWNSBOROUGH, P	Mr. E. JOLLY	1 WARD, Chris
2 FRETWELL, David	(Manchester)	2 LYNE, Kevin
3 COOPER, Ian		3 BAYLISS, Martin
4 OATES, Graham	'AMBERVALE' GUEST HOUSE	4 PUNSHEON, Ralph
5 NAPIER, John	BED BREAKFAST AND EVENING MEAL	5 FRANCIS, Billy
6 COOKE, Joe	REASONABLE TERMS	6 PALMER, Kevin
7 BAKER, Roy	Phone 58067	7 CLEMENTS, David
8 HAM, Bobby		8 LAWRANCE, Ken
9 INGRAM, Gerry	Linesmen: Orange Flag	9 DEEHAN, Kevin
10 JOHNSON, Rod	Mr. T. CARTER (Padiham)	10 HORNE, Arthur
11 BROWN, Ronnie	Red Flag Mr. A. BRADLEY	11 ALLNER, Graham
12 JOHNSTON, John	(Accrington)	12 EDWARDS, C.
Records Loaned by VALLANCES, MARKET STREET, BRADFORD		

BRADFORD CITY
Association Football Club (1908) Limited

Directors:
R. Martin *Chairman*
J. Dunne *Vice-Chairman*
H. B. Metcalfe
K. D. Morrison
J. C. Tordoff
D. W. Wilkinson
Hon. Medical Officer:
Dr. R. Strachan
General Manager and Secretary:
J. Mellor
Team Manager:
G. B. Edwards

F.A. CHALLENGE CUP
3rd ROUND

Souvenir Brochure
5p

Sunday, 6th January 1974—Kick-Off 2-00 p.m.
versus
ALVECHURCH

Above left: Allen Batsford – manager at both Walton and Wimbledon during their stirring cup runs of the 1970s.

Above right and middle: Worcestershire village side Alvechurch were formed in 1929 and hold the record for the longest FA Cup tie in history against Oxford City in 1971/72, needing six matches to decide a fourth-qualifying-round tie. Two days after finally seeing off Oxford they faced Aldershot in the first round and lost 4-2, but they had better luck in 1973/74, beating Exeter and King's Lynn before losing 4-2 at Bradford City in the third round. The club rose to the Southern League before folding in 1992.

Below: Grantham Town – formed in 1874 – had their best run in 1973/74, reaching the third round for the first, and so far only, time. They beat Hillingdon and then, more surprisingly, Third Division Rochdale 5-3 at Spotland after missing their chance in a 1-1 home draw. The Gingerbreads then faced Second Division Middlesbrough, losing 2-0 before a record 6,578 crowd at their old London Road ground.

ROCHDALE—White with Blue and Yellow Sash		GRANTHAM	
POOLE, Mick	1	GARDINER, Chris	
SMITH, Graham	2	BLOOMER, Jimmy	
BRADBURY, Barry	3	CRAWFORD, Andy	
BEBBINGTON, Keith	4	THOMPSON, Colin	
ARNOLD, Steve	5	HARRISON, Ron	
MARSH, Arthur	6	CHAMBERS, Mick	
BROGDEN, Lee	7	HORROBIN, Brent	
TAYLOR, Alan	8	TAYLOR, Gerry	
SKEETE, Leo	9	NIXON, Ernie	
GOWANS, Peter	10	NORRIS, Bob	
DOWNES, Bobby	11	BENSKIN, Denis	
	12	CLAPHAM, Graham	

Referee: M LOWE, Sheffield
Linesmen: J. R. Griffiths, Manchester. Red Flag; J. B. WORRALL, Warrington, Yellow Flag.

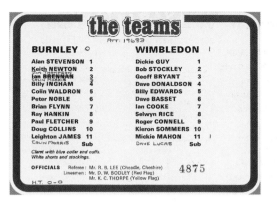

the teams

BURNLEY 0   **WIMBLEDON** 1

ATT: 19683

BURNLEY		WIMBLEDON	
Alan STEVENSON	1	Dickie GUY	1
Keith NEWTON	2	Bob STOCKLEY	2
Ian BRENNAN	3	Geoff BRYANT	3
Billy INGHAM	4	Dave DONALDSON	4
Colin WALDRON	5	Billy EDWARDS	5
Peter NOBLE	6	Dave BASSET	6
Brian FLYNN	7	Ian COOKE	7
Ray HANKIN	8	Selwyn RICE	8
Paul FLETCHER	9	Roger CONNELL	9
Doug COLLINS	10	Kieron SOMMERS	10
Leighton JAMES	11	Mickie MAHON	11
Colin MORRIS	Sub	Dave Lucas	Sub

Claret with blue collar and cuffs.
White shorts and stockings.

OFFICIALS   Referee: Mr. R. B. LEE (Cheadle, Cheshire)
       Linesmen: Mr. D. W. BODLEY (Red Flag)
            Mr. K. C. THORPE (Yellow Flag)   4875

H.T. 0-0

Above left and right: Southern Leaguers Wimbledon caused a real shock by beating First Division Burnley at Turf Moor with a forty-ninth-minute Mick Mahon goal which put the Dons well and truly on the map. The next round saw them at mighty Leeds United, where a dramatic penalty save by Dickie Guy enabled them to leave Elland Road with a 0-0 draw against the reigning champions. A replay at Selhurst Park, watched by 45,701, saw a Dave Bassett own goal finally end the part-timers' dreams.

Right and below: Leatherhead of the Isthmian League were formed in 1946 and did little in the cup until 1974/75, when they made a huge impact, beating Bishop Stortford, and then League clubs Colchester and Brighton, before drawing First Division Leicester. They transferred the game to Filbert Street and stormed into a 2-0 lead. The defining moment of the game is shown as Chris Kelly takes the ball round Mark Wallington in the Foxes' goal, but the angle became tighter, his shot was scrambled off the line and Leicester began their comeback to a narrow victory over the Tanners.

Above and below left: Stafford Rangers were also causing grief for their bigger brothers in the 1974/75 season with victories over Stockport, Halifax and Rotherham – their first giantkillings since their formation in 1876. The fourth round saw them entertain Third Division Peterborough at Stoke, losing 2-1 in front of a huge Victoria Ground crowd of 31,000.

Below right: Roy Dwight (1933-2002), the Erith-born FA Cup winner with Nottingham Forest in 1959. He steered Tooting & Mitcham into the fourth round in 1975/76 as manager before losing out 4-2 to Bradford.

PRIDE OF STAFFORD

ROY CHAPMAN (manager): Joined Rangers in 1970 and during this time Rangers have enjoyed their most successful playing period, Roy played for Aston Villa, Lincoln, Mansfield, Port Vale and Chester before coming to Rangers as player-manager. Scored over 200 goals in League football. Regular member of the Potteries All-Stars along with Ken Jones, Gordon Banks, George Eastham and former Scottish international, Jackie Mudie.

KEN JONES (coach): An inspector in the Staffs County Police Force stationed at H.Q. Stafford, Ken was team manager of the British Police soccer team for three years before joining Rangers this season. Born at Rhos' near Wrexham, he played for the Wrexham schoolboys team that reached the finals of the Welsh Trophy and the English Schools Trophy. Joined Wrexham's groundstaff on leaving school and played for the Welsh club until he was twenty. Transferred to Crystal Palace, he gained three Welsh Under-23 caps and later played for Swindon Town and Rangers.

JIM ARNOLD (goalkeeper): A product of local junior football, he joined the club as an amateur five years ago. Now in his second season as a part-time pro, he works as a local Government Officer with the Staffs County Council. Plays cricket in the close season and is reckoned to be more than useful with both bat and ball. Single but courting, Jim lives in Stafford.

BOB RITCHIE (full-back): Younger brother of Stoke City striker John Ritchie. Joined Rangers three seasons ago as a utility player after spells as an apprentice with Stoke and Arsenal. Works as a sales correspondent. Last season Bob was selected to represent the N.P.L. in a prestige game against Manchester City.

DAVID COOKE (left-back): Joined Rangers at the start of this season from Fleetwood and includes Wolves, Stockport and Bangor among his previous clubs. Works as an insurance inspector and likes playing golf and listening records. Married with two children, David lives at Poulton-le-Fiilde, Blackpool.

BEN SEDDON (centre-half): Joined Rangers in March '74 from Tranmere Rovers. Drives a lorry for a living and lists music as his main interest outside of football. A Liverpudlian, Ben

was recently married and has set up home in Bootle.

MICK MORRIS (sweeper):' Veteran of the side, but his game has been rejuvenated since he came to Rangers three years ago from Port Vale. Previously played for Oxford United. Married with two children, Mick's ambition is to play at Wembley with Rangers. He works for a local shoe firm in Stafford and lives in Stoke-on-Trent.

JIM SARGEANT (midfield): Longest serving member of the club and this season is his benefit year (10 years). Joined Rangers from the local junior league and is a painter and decorator with the Stafford Corporation. He was born in Stafford and lives on one of the towns new estates.

STUART CHAPMAN (midfield): No relation of manager Roy, Geordie Stuart has been nick-named 'Shack' by his teammates. Joined Rangers from Port Vale five years ago. Lists tennis, boxing and music among his interests. Single but courting, 'Shack' lives close to Rangers ground in Marston Road.

TONY KEYES (midfield): Youngest member of the squad and joined the club from Stockport County at the start of the season. Previously had a spell with Manchester United. A plumber by trade, his interests are squash, tennis and golf. Married, Tony lives in Salford.

ROGER JONES (Striker): In his second spell with the club after having seen service with Walsall, Rhyl and Oswestry before returning to Marston Road last season. Married with two boys, Roger works as an instrument tester and lives in Stafford.

MICK CULLERTON (Striker): Joined Rangers from Torquay in 1970 after spending a short time with Derby County. Leading scorer last year with 40, he again heads the Rangers scoring chart with 22. He works as an assembly operator. Married, Mick lives at Cheadle.

HUGH McLEISH (striker): A former Scottish Youth international, He joined Rangers last year after spells with Sunderland, Dundee United and Luton Town. Works as an assembler and is married with three children.

COLIN CHADWICK (winger): In his second year with the club, having joined them from Wigan. He is a contracts representative who likes listening to records in his spare time. Married with one daughter, Colin lives in Stoke-on-Trent.

Roy Dwight

NORTHWICH VICS (Green shirts/black shorts)	OLDHAM ATHLETIC (Blue shirts/white shorts)
1—J. FARMER	J. PLATT— 1
2—K. ECCLESHARE	I. WOOD— 2
3—A. NEMAN	M. WHITTLE— 3
4—L. WAIN	G. BELL— 4
5—G. HAMLETT	K. HICKS— 5
6—K. JONES	J. HURST— 6
7—J. SWEDE	I. ROBINS— 7
8—F. CORRIGAN	D. IRVING— 8
9—P. SMITH	V. HALOM— 9
10—J. KING	L. CHAPMAN—10
11—J. COLLIER	C. VALENTINE—11
Sub.: Stuart Hutchinson	Sub.: Alan Groves

Northwich Victoria – founded in 1874 – were briefly members of the Football League in the Victorian period but made little impact on the cup until 1976/77, when they beat three Football League clubs in a dramatic run that was finally ended in the fourth round by Oldham 3-1 at Maine Road. Earlier they had beaten Rochdale, Peterborough and Watford.

Line-up

Wigan Athletic Blue and White Stripes	Sheffield Wednesday All Yellow
1. J. BROWN	1. C. TURNER
2. K. MORRIS	2. R. WALDEN
3. J. HINNIGAN	3. D. RUSHBURY
4. T. GORE	4. H. DOWD
5. N. WARD	5. D. CUSACK
6. I. GILLIBRAND	6. J. MULLEN
7. M. WHITTLE	7. R. WYLDE
8. M. WORSWICK	8. P. BRADSHAW
9. M. MOORE	9. T. TYNAN
10. J. WILKIE	10. I. PORTERFIELD
11. J. WRIGHT	11. R. HOPE
12. W. STYLES	12. TO BE NAMED

Wigan Athletic were playing their final season as non Leaguers and beat York City in the first round, and then the much bigger Sheffield Wednesday to take their ninth giantkilling scalp. A 4-0 defeat at First Division Birmingham ended their campaign.

Referee:
Mr. N. G. ASHLEY (Nantwich)

Linesmen:
R. D. BAYLEY (Red Flag)
J. J. SHAWCROSS (Orange Flag)

Above: Wycombe Wanderers – formed in 1884 – were a top Isthmian League side for many years without making much impression on the FA Cup. That changed in the seventies: firstly they beat Newport County and then in 1974/75 they surged through to the third round with victories over Cheltenham and Bournemouth, before losing to Middlesbrough 1-0 in a replay. The Chairboys' record goalscorer, Tony Horseman (right), clashes with Boro' defender John Craggs. Four League clubs were beaten in all before Wycombe's rise up the pyramid culminated in their move into the Football League in 1993.

Left: Derek Dougan (1938-2007). The Belfast-born centre forward – never far from controversy – came into the non-League game at the end of a long career that took in Distillery, Portsmouth, Blackburn, Wolves and Leicester before moving to Kettering as player-manager. He scored the only goal to see off Oxford United in 1976/77 – the year they became the first side to put a sponsor's name on a club shirt.

Blyth Spartans produced one of the most famous runs of all time in 1977/78 after starting in the qualifying rounds. The competition proper saw them beat Burscough, Chesterfield, Enfield and Stoke before drawing at Wrexham in the fifth round after the Welsh side scored in the last minute. The replay was moved to St James' Park as the Geordie fans willed their heroes on, but even a 42,137 crowd couldn't quite turn it the Northern Leaguers' way.

Droylsden were formed in 1892 and chalked up their only giantkilling in 1978/79 with a 1-0 win at Rochdale from a David Taylor goal. Fellow non-League side Altrincham beat them 2-0 in the second round.

Coventry Sporting produced a major shock in 1975/76 by toppling Tranmere Rovers 2-0 before losing to Peterborough at the ground of neighbouring Coventry City 4-0. The club – formed as Coventry Amateurs in 1946 – were unable to step up from their brief cup fame and folded in 1989.

Harlow had a memorable centenary year with a first ever cup run that saw them beat Leytonstone, Southend and Leicester in a replay before losing out to Watford in a battling 4-3 defeat. Here Neal Prosser opens the scoring for Harlow – a lead they held into the second half.

Harlow Town in 1979/80 during their great cup run.

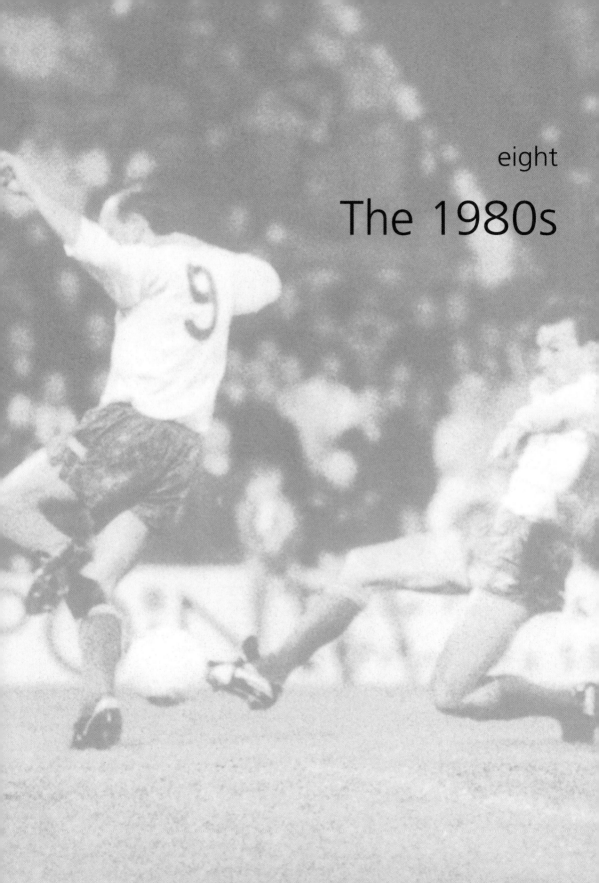

eight

The 1980s

The 1980s firmly established the Alliance Premier League – the Conference from 1986 – as the main threat to Football League clubs. Of the 65 giantkillings in the decade, a massive 47 were achieved by the Conference sides. At long last automatic promotion into the Football League meant a flow of distinguished clubs came onto the non-League scene, with both Lincoln and Darlington achieving giantkillings in their brief one-season sojourn into non-League football.

Telford had a phenomenal decade with ten victims – a record breaking four in a single season as they beat Lincoln, Preston, Bradford City and Darlington in 1984/85. In any other period the eight victories of Altrincham would have topped the tally. Enfield collected five victims, whilst three other sides – Dagenham, Maidstone and Sutton United – all managed trebles.

The number of leagues providing the headline-making heroes had been reduced to just the Isthmian League (eight), the Northern Premier League (six) and the Northern League (four), leaving the Southern League without a single victory.

Giantkillers of the 1980s

(Non-League sides in capitals)

Season	Round				
1980	1	MOSSLEY (NPL)	1	Crewe (FL4)	0
	2	ENFIELD (IL)	2	Hereford United (FL4)	0
	2R	ALTRINCHAM (APL)	1	Scunthorpe United (FL4)	0
	2R	Gillingham (FL3)	0	MAIDSTONE UNITED (APL)	2
	3R	ENFIELD (IL)	3	Port Vale (FL4)	0
1981/82	1	PENRITH (NL)	1	Chester (FL3)	1
	1R	ALTRINCHAM (APL)	3	Sheffield United (FL4)	0
	2	ENFIELD (APL)	4	Wimbledon (FL3)	1
	2R	ALTRINCHAM (APL)	4	York City (FL4)	3
1982/83	1	ALTRINCHAM (APL)	2	Rochdale (FL4)	1
	1	BOSTON UNITED (APL)	3	Crewe (FL4)	1
	1	Halifax Town (FL4)	0	NORTH SHIELDS (NL)	1
	1	SLOUGH (IL)	1	Millwall (FL3)	0
	1	Reading (FL3)	1	BISHOP STORTFORD (IL)	2
	1R	NORTHWICH VICTORIA (APL)	3	Chester (FL4)	1
	1R	TELFORD UNITED (APL)	2	Wigan Athletic (FL3)	1
	2	Cardiff City (FL3)	2	WEYMOUTH (APL)	3
	2	WORCESTER CITY (APL)	2	Wrexham (FL3)	1
1983/84	1	Halifax Town (FL4)	2	WHITBY TOWN (NL)	3
	1	TELFORD UNITED (APL)	1	Stockport County (FL4)	0
	1R	MAIDSTONE UNITED (APL)	2	Exeter City (FL3)	1
	1R	WORCESTER CITY (APL)	2	Aldershot (FL4)	1
	2R	TELFORD UNITED (APL)	3	Northampton (FL4)	2
	3	Rochdale (FL4)	3	TELFORD UNITED (APL)	4
1984/85	1	Blackpool (FL4)	0	ALTRICHAM (APL)	1
	1	NORTHWICH VICTORIA (APL)	3	Crewe (FL4)	1
	1R	BOGNOR REGIS (IL)	3	Swansea (FL3)	1
	1R	ENFIELD (APL)	3	Exeter (FL4)	0
	1R	Swindon (FL4)	1	DAGENHAM (APL)	2
	1R	TELFORD UNITED (APL)	2	Lincoln City (FL3)	1
	2	Aldershot (FL4)	0	BURTON ALBION (NPL)	2
	2	DAGENHAM (APL)	2	Peterborough Utd (FL4)	0
	2	Preston (FL3)	1	TELFORD UNITED (APL)	4
	3	TELFORD UNITED (APL)	2	Bradford City (FL3)	1
	4R	TELFORD UNITED (APL)	3	Darlington (FL4)	0
1985/86	1	DAGENHAM (APL)	2	Cambridge Utd (FL4)	1
	1	Stockport County (FL4)	0	TELFORD UTD (APL)	1
	1	WYCOMBE WANDERERS (APL)	2	Colchester Utd (FL4)	0

	2	Blackpool (FL3)	1	ALTRINCHAM (APL)	2
	2	Hartlepool (FL4)	0	FRINKLEY ATHLETIC (APL)	1
	3	Birmingham (FL1)	1	ALTRINCHAM (APL)	2
1986/87	1	CAERNARVON (NPL)	1	Stockport (FL4)	0
	1	TELFORD UTD (CON)	3	Burnley (FL4)	0
	1R	CHORLEY (NPL)	3	Wolves (FL4)	0
	2	MAIDSTONE UTD (CON)	1	Cambridge Utd (FL4)	0
	2R	York City (FL3)	1	CAERNARVON (NPL)	2
1987/88	1	Chester (FL3)	0	RUNCORN (CON)	1
	1	LINCOLN CITY (CON)	2	Crewe (FL4)	1
	1	MACCLESFIELD (CON)	4	Carlisle (FL4)	2
	1	SUTTON UNITED (CON)	3	Aldershot (FL3)	0
	2	Cambridge United (FL4)	0	YEOVIL (IL)	1
	2	MACCLESFIELD (CON)	4	Rotherham (FL3)	0
	2	Peterborough United (FL4)	1	SUTTON UTD (CON)	3
1988/89	1	ALTRINCHAM (CON)	3	Lincoln (FL4)	2
	1	BOGNOR REGIS (IL)	2	Exeter (FL4)	1
	1R	Wrexham (FL4)	2	RUNCORN (CON)	3
	1R	Leyton Orient (FL4)	0	ENFIELD (CON)	1
	2	KETTERING (CON)	2	Bristol Rovers (FL3)	1
	3	SUTTON UNITED (CON)	2	Coventry City (FL1)	1
	3R	Halifax Town (FL4)	2	KETTERING (CON)	3
1989/90	1	AYLESBURY UTD (IL)	1	Southend Utd (FL4)	0
	1	Scarborough (FL4)	0	WHITLEY BAY (NPL)	1
	1R	WELLING UTD (CON)	1	Gillingham (FL4)	0
	2	DARLINGTON (CON)	3	Halifax (FL4)	0
	2	WHITLEY BAY (NPL)	2	Preston (FL3)	0

TEAMS

CHANGES	GILLINGHAM		MAIDSTONE	CHANGES
	RON HILLYARD	1	DICKIE GUY	
	JOHN SHARPE	2	BRIAN THOMPSON	
	ANDY FORD	3	CHRIS KINNEAR	
	JOHN OVERTON	4	KENNY HILL	
	MARK WEATHERLY	5	JOHN HUTTON	
	JOHN CRABBE	6	STEVE HAMBERGER	
	TERRY NICHOLL	7	JOHN DAUBNEY	
	TONY BOTTIGLIERI	8	FRANK OVARD	
	KEN PRICE	9	ANDY WOON	
	DANNY WESTWOOD	10	GLENN AITKEN	
	DEAN WHITE	11	MARK NEWSON	
		12		

Previous and above: Maidstone United won the Kent derby with Third Division Gillingham in a three-match saga in 1980 after taking three games to beat fellow Alliance Leaguers Kettering in the first round. Frank Ovard scored the clincher. The third round saw them face Exeter at home and stumble out 4-2.

Enfield's ever-growing reputation as cup battlers reached its height in 1980/81 with a trip to the fourth round. Wembley, Hereford and Port Vale were all seen off and a trip to Oakwell to take on Third Division Barnsley could have gone even better than a 1-1 draw. Here Ronnie Howell and Peter Burton argue with referee Peter Willis after a goal has been disallowed. Unfortunately, the replay at White Hart Lane saw Barnsley win 3-0 in front of a 35,244 crowd.

Altrincham reached the third round for a fourth successive season, beating Sheffield United and York before rather surprisingly suffering a 6-1 reverse at Third Division Burnley.

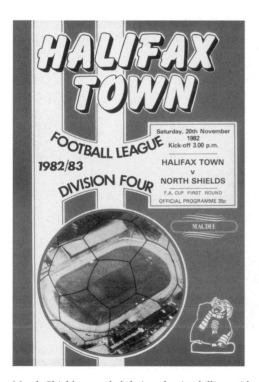

HALIFAX TOWN
1. Lee SMELT
2. Keith NOBBS
3. Mick WOOD
4. Dave EVANS
5. Tony SMITH
6. Paul HENDRIE
7. Dave STANIFORTH
8. Bobby DAVISON
9. Vernon ALLATT
10. Steve SPOONER
11. Malcolm GOODMAN
12. Stephen WARD

NORTH SHIELDS
1. Tony HARRISON
2. John WATERSON
3. George DICKSON
4. David VARTY
5. Jimmy HARMISON
6. Ray YOUNG
7. Geoff SMITH
8. Bobby DOIG
9. Paul ROSS
10. Ian DONALDSON
11. Bede McCAFFREY
12. Steven WRIGHT

North Shields recorded their only giantkilling with a 1-0 win at Fourth Division Halifax courtesy of a Bede McCaffrey goal. Walsall beat them 3-0 at Appleby Park in the second round. First formed in 1898 and reformed twice, in 1928 and 1992, the club are currently members of the Northern League.

Above left: Whitby Town achieved their only success against Fourth Division Halifax in 1983/84 with a fine 3-2 win at the Shay. The next round saw them lose narrowly to Wigan 1-0. Pictured is Derek Hampton firing home the first goal in the 3-2 win at Halifax as Phil Linacre looks on. Formed in 1926, they are currently members of the Northern Premier League.

Above right: Chorley were founded in 1883 and had to wait until 1986 for a giantkilling, but when it came it was spectacular, with Wolves being beaten 3-0 after two drawn games. The programme cover shows Paul Moss scoring in the first game.

Telford United – formerly Wellington Town – were formed in 1876, changing their name to Telford in 1970. It was a 1982/83 first-round victory over Third Division Wigan that set them off on an amazing series of triumphs over their big brothers and just four seasons later they had collected an incredible ten scalps – by far the most intense cull of Football League clubs in FA Cup history. The 1983/84 team are pictured.

TEAMS

BIRMINGHAM CITY
Colours:
Blue Shirts, Red/White
Flashes. White Shorts

ALTRINCHAM
Colours:

Birmingham City	#	Altrincham
DAVID SEAMAN	1	JEFF WEALANDS
RAY RANSON	2	ELFYN EDWARDS
BRIAN ROBERTS	3	PETER DENSMORE
JIM HAGAN	4	JEFF JOHNSON
KENNY ARMSTRONG	5	PAUL CUDDY
MARTIN KUHL	6	MIKE FARRELLY
DES BREMNER	7	DOUG NEWTON
BILLY WRIGHT	8	JOHN DAVISON
ANDREW KENNEDY	9	PAUL REID
MARK JONES	10	COLIN CHESTERS
ROBERT HOPKINS	11	GARY ANDERSON
	12	PETER CONNING

Altrincham collected their twelfth League scalp with a 2–1 win at First Division Birmingham.

Caernarfon Town produced their best run in 1986/87, beating Stockport and York to add to their only previous giantkilling of Darlington in 1929/30. It also took Barnsley two bites of the cherry to finally see them off 1–0 at Oakwell. The club are currently members of the Welsh League.

Lincoln City became the first team to suffer automatic relegation from the Football League in 1987/88 but they gained instant promotion. To cap a memorable single season in non-League they also had a good cup run, beating Fourth Division Crewe 2-1 before losing out 4-3 at Mansfield.

Enfield recorded a seventh giantkilling in 1988/89 after a marathon three-match saga with Leyton Orient. Here Robin Lewis crashes in the only goal.

Sutton United became the sixth non-League side to beat a First Division side with a dramatic 2-1 victory over Coventry at Gander Green Lane. They joined Colchester, who beat Huddersfield in 1947/48; Yeovil, who defeated Sunderland in 1948/49; Hereford, who triumphed over Newcastle in 1971/72; Burnley, who beat Wimbledon in 1974/75; and Birmingham, who disposed of Altrincham in 1985/86.

Above right: Barry Williams, the Sutton manager who became a personality in his own right during the cup run.

Above left: Matthew Hanlon (second right) scores the winner for Sutton versus Coventry before the run came to an end with an 8-0 thrashing from another First Division side, Norwich.

Darlington emulated Lincoln two years earlier by bouncing back after relegation from the Football League in a single season. They had a good cup run as well, reaching the third round by beating Northwich and Fourth Division Halifax before bowing out 3-1 in a replay to Fourth Division Cambridge United.

Whitley Bay – formed in 1897 – had to wait until 1989 for their first trip into the competition proper, but it was well worth the wait as the Northern Premier Leaguers first beat Fourth Division Scarborough 1-0 at Seamer Road then, in front of the *Match of the Day* cameras, beat Third Division Preston 2-0 at Hillheads Park. Pictured is Peter Robinson firing home the first goal.

A flurry of champagne as Whitley Bay celebrate beating Preston and dream of a third-round game with Liverpool or Manchester United. Like so many clubs before and since, they were brought down to earth when the draw was made at Lancaster Gate, away to Rochdale, resulting in a 1-0 defeat.

nine

The 1990s

The 1990s won't go down as one of the more successful periods for non-League sides with a tally of only 61 giantkillings – slightly down on the previous period.

The major change of the period came in 1992 with the introduction of the Premier League and the re-labelling of the divisions below.

Predictably, the Conference dominated in the victory stakes with 38, whilst the Isthmian League managed 13, the Southern League made a return with five, the Northern Premier League four and there was a single victory for the Northern League. Club-wise, Yeovil managed five wins – just in front of Enfield, Hednesford and Woking.

Giantkillers of the 1990s

(Non-League sides in capitals)

1990/91	1	CHORLEY (NPL)	2	Bury (FL3)	1
	1	COLCHESTER UTD (CON)	2	Reading (FL3)	1
	1	Scarborough (FL4)	0	LEEK TOWN (NPL)	2
	2R	Northampton (FL4)	0	BARNET (CON)	1
	3	West Brom (FL2)	2	WOKING (IL)	4
1991/92	1	Aldershot (FL4)	0	ENFIELD (IL)	1
	1	CRAWLEY TOWN (SL)	4	Northampton (FL3)	2
	1	Fulham (FL3)	0	HAYES (IL)	2
	1R	Halifax Town (FL4)	1	WITTON ALBION (CON)	2
	1R	TELFORD UTD (CON)	2	Stoke City (FL3)	1
	1R	Walsall (FL4)	0	YEOVIL (CON)	1
	2	Maidstone United (FL4)	1	KETTERING (CON)	2
	2R	FARNBOROUGH (CON)	4	Torquay United (FL3)	3
1992/93	1	Cardiff City (FL3)	2	BATH CITY (CON)	3
	1	MARINE (NPL)	4	Halifax (FL3)	1
	1	Torquay United (FL3)	2	YEOVIL (CON)	5
	1R	ALTRINCHAM (CON)	2	Chester (FL2)	0
	1R	STAFFORD RANGERS (CON)	2	Lincoln (FL3)	1
	2R	Hereford Utd (FL3)	1	YEOVIL (CON)	2
1993/94	1	Colchester Utd (FL3)	3	SUTTON UNITED (IL)	4
	1	HALIFAX TOWN (CON)	2	West Bromwich Albion (FL1)	1
	1	MACCLESFIELD (CON)	2	Hartlepool Utd (FL2)	0
	1	Northampton (FL3)	1	BROMSGROVE ROVERS (CON)	2
	1	YEOVIL (CON)	1	Fulham (FL2)	0
	1R	NUNEATON BOROUGH (SL)	2	Swansea (FL2)	1
	2	BATH CITY (CON)	2	Hereford Utd (FL3)	1
	2	Torquay Utd (FL3)	0	SUTTON UNITED (IL)	1
	3	Birmingham (FL1)	1	KIDDERMINSTER (CON)	2
	4	KIDDERMINSTER (CON)	1	Preston (FL3)	0
1994/95	1	ENFIELD (CON)	1	Cardiff City (FL2)	0
	1	KINGSTONIAN (IL)	2	Brighton (FL2)	1
	1	MARLOW (IL)	2	Oxford Utd (FL2)	0
	1R	HITCHIN (IL)	4	Hereford Utd (FL3)	2
	2	ALTRINCHAM (CON)	1	Wigan Athletic (FL3)	0
	2R	Torquay Utd (FL3)	0	ENFIELD (IL)	1
1995/96	1	Bury (FL3)	0	BLYTH SPARTANS (NPL)	2
	1	WOKING (CON)	1	Barnet (FL3)	0
	1	GRAVESEND (SL)	2	Colchester Utd (FL3)	0
	1R	HITCHIN (IL)	2	Bristol Rovers (FL2)	1
1996/97	1R	Brighton (FL3)	1	SUDBURY (SL)	1
	1R	Millwall (FL3)	0	WOKNG (CON)	1
	2	Blackpool (FL2)	0	HEDNESFORD (CON)	1
	2	Cambridge Utd (FL3)	0	WOKING (CON)	2
	2	Leyton Orient (FL3)	1	STEVENAGE (CON)	2
	3	HEDNESFORD TOWN (CON)	1	York City (FL2)	0

1997/98	1	HEREFORD UNITED (CON)	2	Brighton (FL3)		1
	1	Hull City (FL3)	0	HEDNESFORD (CON)		2
	1R	BASINGSTOKE TOWN (IL)	2	Wycombe (FL2)		2
	1R	Leyton Orient (FL3)	0	HENDON (IL)		1
	2R	STEVENAGE BOROUGH (CON)	2	Cambridge Utd (FL3)		1
	3	Swindon Town (FL1)	1	STEVENAGE (CON)		2
1998/99	1	BEDLINGTON TERRIERS (NL)	4	Colchester Utd (FL2)		1
	1	HEDNESFORD TOWN (CON)	3	Barnet (FL3)		1
	1	RUSHDEN & DIAMONDS (CON)	1	Shrewsbury (FL3)		0
	1	Southend United (FL3)	0	DONCASTER (CON)		1
	2	Mansfield Town (FL3)	1	SOUTHPORT (CON)		2
	2	YEOVIL (CON)	2	Northampton (FL2)		0
1999/2000	1	Chesterfield (FL2)	1	ENFIELD (IL)		2
	1	ILKESTON TOWN (SL)	2	Carlisle United (FL3)		1
	1	HEREFORD UNITED (CON)	1	York City (FL3)		0
	2	HEREFORD UNITED (CON)	1	Hartlepool United (FL3)		0

Woking had never beaten a Football League club until 1990/91, when the Isthmian Leaguers began to gain a reputation as a club on the rise. The opening two rounds saw them beat Conference sides Merthyr and Kidderminster before taking on West Brom at the Hawthorns, beating them 4-2. A narrow 1-0 defeat at Everton in the fourth round ended their best ever run. Pictured is Tim Buzaglo outpacing Graham Roberts and Gary Strodder on the way to scoring at West Brom.

Above: Substitute Terry Worsfield scores the fourth Woking goal amid dejected Albion defenders.

Left and below: Two heroes of the cup run – Tim Buzaglo and Derek Brown.

Above: Leek Town were formed in 1946 and had their most successful period around 1990 with an FA Trophy final appearance and a surprise cup win at Fourth Division Scarborough, with goals from Alan Somerville and Dave Sutton. A 4-0 defeat at Third Division Chester ended their run.

Below left: Colchester United were back as non-Leaguers after a forty-year gap and beat Reading 2-1 before going down 4-1 to Leyton Orient in a replay.

Below right: Farnborough Town were only formed in 1967 and progressed rapidly. They made a big impression in the FA Cup in 1991/92, beating Halesowen and then Torquay in a dramatic game by 4-3. This provided them with a plum home tie with West Ham. They switched the fixture from Cherrywood Road to Upton Park and gained a creditable 1-1 draw, returning to give another battling display in the replay, which they lost 1-0. Pictured is long-serving manager Ted Pearce celebrating with the team after beating Torquay.

COLCHESTER UTD.	V	LEYTON ORIENT
SCOTT BARRETT	1	PAUL HEALD
TONY ENGLISH	2	STEVE BAKER
IAN ATKINS	3	TERRY HOWARD
EAMONN COLLINS	4	CHRIS ZORICICH
SCOTT DANIELS	5	ADRIAN WHITBREAD
NEALE MARMON	6	GEOFF PIKE
WARREN DONALD	7	DANNY CARTER
GARY BENNETT	8	STEVE CASTLE
MARK YATES	9	KEVIN NUGENT
MARIO WALSH	10	LEE HARVEY
NICKY SMITH	11	KENNY ACHAMPONG
ROY McDONOUGH	12	GREG BERRY
MIKE MASTERS	14	KEVIN DICKENSON

Referee:
ROGER WISEMAN
(Boreham Wood)

Linesmen:
W. M. JORDAN   J. C. SMITH   Reserve Official:
(Pinner)   (Wealdstone)   M. CROUCHMAN
(White Roding)

Crawley Town were formed in 1896 and, after folding, reformed in 1938. They produced their only giantkilling to date in 1991/92, beating Northampton 4-2 at Town Mead. They then won 2-0 at Hayes before meeting fellow Sussex side Brighton in the third round, losing 5-0 at the Goldstone. Pictured is Craig Whittington about to score the first of his two goals.

Cliff Cant rifles home the equaliser for Crawley against Northampton.

Marine, the Crosby, Liverpool-based club, were formed in 1894 and have beaten two Football League clubs through the years: Barnsley in 1975/76 and Halifax in 1992/93 with an emphatic 4-1 scoreline. A 3-2 victory in the next round over Stafford Rangers put them into the third round but the dream tie failed to materialise and they lost 3-1 at Crewe. Pictured is Graham Rowlands putting Halifax goalkeeper Lee Bracey under pressure.

Chris Camden celebrates after Graham Rowlands puts Marine 3-0 up against Halifax in 1992/93.

Left: Roly Howard, the long-serving and successful Marine manager from 1972–2005.

Middle: A Huish Park record crowd of 8,612 saw Arsenal triumph 3–1 on their way to winning the coveted trophy. Andy Wallace is pictured taking on Ian Wright and Alan Smith.

Below: Hereford were on the receiving end the following season as Bath celebrated. Paul Batty (with cup in hand) scored the winner and goalkeeper David Mogg (next to him) produced a fine display.

Kidderminster Harriers were formed in 1886 and had a long wait for cup fame. When it finally came in 1993/94 it was something special as they became only the fifth non-League team to reach the fifth round of the cup, following in the footsteps of Colchester, Yeovil, Blyth and Telford. Fellow Conference sides Kettering and Woking were beaten in the opening two rounds; then came a 2-1 victory at Birmingham with goalscorers Neil Cartwright and Jon Purdie celebrating their great achievement.

The fourth round saw Delwyn Humphreys score the only goal to send Preston toppling. The fifth round provided a plum tie with West Ham at Aggborough. Harriers won promotion to the Football League in 2000 – a place they lost in 2006.

Marlow were one of the fifteen original entrants to the FA Cup in 1871/72 and, apart from a single season, have entered each year with success thin on the ground. The 1990s saw a change for the better with two trips through to the third round. In 1992/93 they beat fellow non-Leaguers Salisbury and VS Rugby before hitting the jackpot with a third-round tie at Tottenham, where they put up a creditable show before losing 5-1. Two years later they beat Second Division Oxford United 2-0, with John Caeser (pictured) scoring the first goal.

Left: Joe O'Connor – record scorer for Hednesford and key player in the cup run, scoring both goals against Middlesbrough, and the winners against Southport and York.

Middle: Gravesend & Northfleet collected their third scalp in 1995/96 with a 2-0 victory over Colchester. A 3-0 replay win over Cinderford saw them through to a third-round tie with Aston Villa, where a 3-0 defeat ended their run.

Above: Alan Shearer was just one of the many stars Stevenage had to contend with in two fourth-round tussles, finally decided at St James' Park in Newcastle's favour 2-1.

Below left: Mark Smith was outstanding for Stevenage in central defence during the cup run and played more than 300 games for them.

Below right: Paul Fairclough was an outstanding manager for Stevenage, steering them to the Conference title and two long cup runs. He later took Barnet into the Football League and managed England's semi-pro international side.

Opposite below: Hednesford Town achieved their greatest success in 1995/97 with a excellent run to the fourth round, where they gave Middlesbrough a big fright before going down 3-2, having beaten Southport, Blackpool and York in the three previous rounds. The team line-up before the home fans at Ayresome Park was, from left to right, back row: Joe O'Conner, Andy Comyn, Tony Hemmings, Stuart Lake, Steve Essex, Scott Cooksey, Colin Lambert, Garry Fitzpatrick, Keith Russell, Richard Dardy. Front row: Wayne Simpson, Paul Carty, Tyrone Street, Bernard McNally, Steve Devine, Kevin Collins, David Harnett.

Bedlington Terriers were formed in 1949 as Bedlington Mechanics and later Bedlington United. The Northern Leaguers became the Terriers in 1974 and certainly lived up to that name in 1998/99. when they crushed Colchester United of the Second Division 4-1. In the second round they battled hard before losing 2-0 at Scunthorpe. From left to right, back row: Keith Perry (manager), Andy Bowes, Archie Gourlay, John Sokolouk, Andy Gowans, Craig Melrose, John Egan, Paul O'Connor, Glen Renforth, Tony Lowery (assistant manager), John Nicholson, Ritchie Bond. Front row: Mark Cameron, Mel Harmison, Dean Gibb, Gary Middleton, Lee Ludlow, Warren Teasdale, Mickey Cross, Martin Pike, Steve Boon.

Left: John Milner, the high-scoring Bedlington forward who helped blitz Colchester with two goals in the 4-1 victory.

ten

The New Century

A record-breaking 13 giantkillings brought something of a false dawn to the new decade. With more of the top non-League sides going full-time, the gap between the Football League and Conference looked narrower than ever. One fact overlooked was that the advent of so many foreign players at the top level had pushed good-quality players further down the Football League and it was soon evident that the teams near the bottom of the League were benefiting from this. As such, the giantkilling tailed off somewhat with the last season covered by this book producing just two. Ironically, one of the victims was Yeovil Town – the greatest of all giantkillers were now a Football League side and the boot was suddenly on the other foot.

Giantkillers of the 2000s

(Non-League sides in capitals)

Season	Round	Home			Away	
2000/01	1	Brentford (FL2)	1		KINGSTONIAN (CON)	3
	1	Halifax Town (FL3)	0		GATESHEAD (NPL)	2
	1	YEOVIL TOWN (CON)	5		Colchester Utd (FL2)	1
	1R	Port Vale (FL2)	1		CANVEY ISLAND (IL)	2
	1R	NUNEATON BOROUGH (CON)	1		Stoke City (FL2)	0
	1R	Hull City (FL3)	0		KETTERING (CON)	1
	1R	NORTHWICH VICTORIA (CON)	1		Bury (FL2)	0
	1R	Plymouth Argyle (FL3)	1		CHESTER CITY (CON)	2
	2	CHESTER CITY (CON)	3		Oxford Utd (FL2)	2
	2	Lincoln City (FL3)	0		DAGENHAM & REDBRIDGE (CON)	1
	2	MORECAMBE (CON)	2		Cambridge Utd (FL2)	1
	2	Blackpool (FL2)	0		YEOVIL (CON)	1
	3	Southend United (FL3)	0		KINGSTONIAN (CON)	1
2001/02	1	Wigan Athletic (FL2)	0		CANVEY ISLAND (IL)	1
	1R	DAGENHAM & REDBRIDGE (CON)	3		Exeter City (FL3)	0
	2	CANVEY ISLAND (IL)	1		Northampton (FL2)	0
2002/03	1	Chesterfield (FL3)	1		MORECAMBE (CON)	2
	1	Colchester United (FL2)	0		CHESTER CITY (CON)	1
	1	MARGATE (CON)	1		Leyton Orient (FL3)	0
	1R	SOUTHPORT (CON)	4		Notts County (FL2)	2
	1R	Queens Park Rangers (FL2)	1		VAUXHALL MOTORS (NPL)	1
	3	Darlington (FL3)	2		FARNBOROUGH (CON)	3
	3R	DAGENHAM & REDBRIDGE (CON)	2		Plymouth (FL2)	0
2003/04	1	HORNCHURCH (IL)	2		Darlington (FL2)	0
	1	SCARBOROUGH (CON)	1		Doncaster Rovers (FL3)	0
	1	STEVENAGE BOROUGH (CON)	2		Stockport County (FL2)	1
	1	Torquay United (FL3)	1		BURTON ALBION (CON)	2
	1	ACCRINGTON STANLEY (CON)	1		Huddersfield (FL1)	0
	2	TELFORD UNITED (CON)	3		Brentford (FL1)	0
	2	Port Vale (FL2)	0		SCARBOROUGH (CON)	1
	2R	ACCRINGTON STANLEY (CON)	0		Bournemouth (FL1)	0
	3	Crewe (FL3)	0		TELFORD UTD (CON)	1
	3R	SCARBOROUGH (CON)	1		Southend Utd (FL1)	0
2004/05	1	EXETER CITY (CON)	1		Grimsby (FL2)	0
	1	HALIFAX TOWN (CON)	3		Cambridge Utd (FL2)	1
	1	HINCKLEY UNITED (CON)	2		Torquay Utd (FL2)	0
	1	HISTON (SL)	2		Shrewsbury (FL2)	0
	1	SLOUGH (IL)	2		Walsall (FL1)	1
	1R	CARLISLE UTD (CON)	1		Bristol Rovers (FL2)	0
	2	EXETER CITY (CON)	2		Doncaster (FL2)	1
2005/06	1	Bournemouth (FL2)	1		TAMWORTH (CON)	1
	1	BURSCOUGH (NPL)	3		Gillingham (FL1)	2
	1R	BURTON ALBION (CON)	1		Peterborough (FL2)	0
	2	Hartlepool Utd (FL2)	1		TAMWORTH (CON)	2
2006/07	1	RUSHDEN & DIAMONDS (CON)	3		Yeovil (FL1)	1
	1	Chesterfield (FL3)	0		BASINGSTOKE TOWN (CON)	1

Right: Kingstonian were formed in 1885 but had to wait until 1994/95 for their first giantkilling, when they beat Brighton 2-1. Gaining promotion to the Conference, they became even stronger and in 2000/01 they went through to the fourth round. Eddie Akuamoah is pictured after scoring the only goal to knock out Southend at Roots Hall. Brentford and Southport had already been defeated but Bristol City beat Kingstonian in a replay. Sadly, the Surrey side suffered a sharp decline with financial problems the following season and are still to recover their old status.

Below: Neil Gregory celebrates scoring the only goal of the game in front of the live *Match of the Day* cameras to see Canvey Island beat Northampton in the 2001/02 competition. Neil had already scored the only goal to see off Wigan in the previous round. Burnley ended their run 4-1 at Turf Moor in the third round.

Left: Chris Kinnear not only had a long and distinguished career as a non-League player, but was successful as a manager with Dover and Margate, his cup highlight being the 1-0 victory over Leyton Orient in 2002/03 whilst with Margate.

Below: Alvin McDonald managed Vauxhall Motors to an unlikely win over Queens Park Rangers at Loftus Road in a first-round replay in 2002/03 on penalties. He later moved on to manage Marine.

Right: The match programme from the goalless first game played at neutral Chester City.

Below: Farnborough had a dream run in 2002/03. After victories over non-League sides in the first two rounds, they were desperately disappointed with a third-round draw away to Darlington. Manager Graham Westley convinced the Conference side that they could win it, giving themselves an even better chance of a glamour tie in the fourth round, and that is exactly what they did. A 3-2 win at Feethams was followed by a tie with Arsenal which was transferred from Cherrywood Road to Highbury, where they were beaten 5-1 but had a financial windfall. Sadly, the team went into liquidation in 2007.

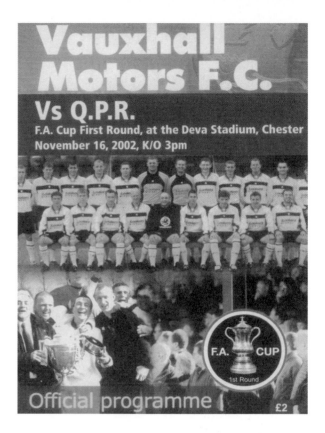

Hornchurch were formed in 1923 and waited eighty years to reach the first round proper, where they made an instant impression by beating Darlington 2-0. They then outplayed Tranmere in the second round, but Rovers had the sort of luck any team needs to have a good run and defeated them, going on to reach the sixth round. Sadly, the following year the Urchins' main benefactor hit financial troubles and the club went to the wall. The team are pictured at the start of the successful 2003/04 season.

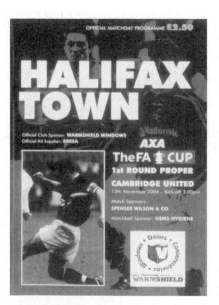

Above left: Halifax Town were formed in 1911 and, following their election to the Football League in 1921, were knocked out by non-Leaguers on 13 occasions. So it was good for them to be able to turn the tables once they became Conference members, beating West Brom and Cambridge United.

Above right: Histon made rapid strides in the early years of the new century after having played in the backwaters since their 1904 formation. They beat Shrewsbury 2-0 before being halted in the second round by Yeovil in 2004/05, and in 2007 they reached the Conference.

Right: Exeter City slipped into non-League football in 2003 – ninety-nine years after their formation – and had a great run in 2004/05, culminating in two clashes with Manchester United in the third round. To achieve this they had to beat Grimsby and Doncaster Rovers. The following season Burton Albion also held Manchester United to a draw before losing out 5-0 at Old Trafford. For both teams it was a financial jackpot that only the FA cup can provide.

Kyle Storer strokes home the penalty that gives Tamworth a 2-1 victory at Bournemouth in the first round of the 2005/06 competition.

FA Cup 1st Round
BURSCOUGH v GILLINGHAM
Saturday 5th November 2005   Kick-off 3.00pm
Match Sponsor: Westbury Homes

BURSCOUGH (Green)	GILLINGHAM (Blue/White)	Squad No.
1. Matthew Boswell	1. Tony Bullock	(17)
2. Andy Barlow	2. Tom Williams	(3)
3. Martin Crowder	3. Paul Smith	(4)
4. Karl Bell	4. Ian Cox	(6)
5. Adam Tong	5. Andrew Crofts	(7)
6. Matthew Parry	6. Andy Hessenthaler	(8)
7. Tony Gray	7. Michael Flynn	(10)
8. Liam Blakeman	8. Chris Hope	(18)
9. Paul Gedman	9. Neil Harris	(19)
10. David Eaton	10. Matthew Jarvis	(21)
11. Ryan Bowen	11. Jon Wallis	(23)
12. Mark Byrne	12. Mark Saunders	(15)
14. Dave Rowan	14. Richard Rose	(16)
15. Jeff Underwood	15. Mark Corneille	(24)
16. Steve Hussey	16. Frannie Collin	(28)
17. David Newnes (g/k)	17. Paul Crichton (g/k)	(1)

Manager: Derek Goulding
Assistant: Chris Stammers

Manager: Neale Cooper
Assistant: Ronnie Jepson

Referee: G.Salisbury (Preston)

Assistants: D.Roberts (Salford), G.T.Stott (Manchester)
Fourth Official: C.N.Harwood

Left: Burscough collected their first Football League scalp with an unlikely victory over Gillingham in 2005/06 after trailing 2-1 with only minutes to go. They lost out to Burton Albion for the prize of playing Manchester United in the next round.

Below: Matt Warner wheels away in delight after scoring the twenty-fifth-minute goal that proved enough for Conference South Basingstoke Town to beat Chesterfield at Saltergate in 2006/07. They lost out to local rivals Aldershot in the second round.

Matt Redmile climbs highest to score the winner for Tamworth at Hartlepool in the second round. The reward was a trip to Stoke, where the First Division side needed two hard-fought games to beat them. Tamworth again reached the third round in 2006/07 without beating a Football League side, but were relegated from the Conference.

Roll of Honour

The full list of giantkillings by non-League clubs between 1925/26 and 2006/07.

19 YEOVIL TOWN
15 ALTRINCHAM
13 TELFORD UNITED
11 ENFIELD
10 HEREFORD UNITED
9 SCARBOROUGH
9 WIGAN ATHLETIC
8 BATH CITY
8 KETERING TOWN
8 PETERBOROUGH UNITED
7 RHYL
6 BEDFORD TOWN
6 BLYTH SPARTANS
6 DAGENHAM & REDBRIDGE
6 MARGATE
6 NORTHWICH VICTORIA
6 SOUTH SHIELDS
5 BOSTON UNITED

5 RUNCORN
5 NUNEATON BOROUGH
5 SCUNTHORPE UNITED
5 SUTTON UNITED
5 WALTHAMSTOW AVENUE
5 WORCESTER CITY
5 WORKINGTON
4 BURTON ALBION
4 STAFFORD RANGERS
4 STEVENAGE BOROUGH
4 COLCHESTER UNITED
4 GAINSBOROUGH TRINITY
4 GATESHEAD
4 HEDNESFORD TOWN
4 LEATHERHEAD
4 MAIDSTONE UNITED
4 MACCLESFIELD TOWN
4 WEYMOUTH
3 BISHOP AUCKLAND
3 CAERNARFON TOWN
3 CANVEY ISLAND
3 CARLISLE UNITED
3 CHELMSFORD CITY
3 DARTFORD
3 FOLKESTONE
3 GILLINGHAM
3 GRAVESEND & NORTHFLEET
3 GUILDFORD CITY
3 KINGSTONIAN
3 NEW BRIGHTON
3 MORECAMBE
3 TAMWORTH
3 TOOTING MITCHAM
3 WYCOMBE WANDERERS
3 CHESTER CITY
3 WOKING
2 ALDERSHOT
2 BANGOR CITY
2 BARNET
2 BASINGSTOKE TOWN
2 BOGNOR REGIS TOWN
2 BURTON TOWN
2 CHORLEY
2 CORINTHIANS
2 EXETER CITY
2 FARNBOROUGH
2 GRANTHAM
2 HALIFAX TOWN
2 HARLOW TOWN
2 HAYES

2 HEADINGTON UNITED
2 HENDON
2 HILLINGDON BOROUGH
2 HITCHIN
2 KIDDERMINSTER HARRIERS
2 KING'S LYNN
2 LEYTONSTONE
2 MARINE
2 MANSFIELD TOWN
2 RUSHDEN DIAMONDS
2 SLOUGH
2 SPENNYMOOR UNITED
2 SOUTHPORT
2 WALTON HERSHAM
2 WHITLEY BAY
2 WIMBLEDON
2 WORKSOP TOWN

The following have achieved one giantkilling:

ACCRINGTON STANLEY, ALVECHURCH, ASHINGTON, AYLESBURY, BARKING, BEDLINGTON TERRIERS BISHOP STORTFORD, BRENTWOOD, BROMSGROVE ROVERS, BURSCOUGH, BUXTON, CAMBRIDGE UNITED, CHILTON COLLIERY CHELTENHAM, CLAPTON, CORBY TOWN, COVENTRY SPORTING, CRAWLEY TOWN, CROOK TOWN, DARLINGTON, DARWEN, DONCASTER ROVERS, DOVER, DROYLESDON, FINCHLEY, FRICKLEY ATHLETIC, GOOLE TOWN, GREAT YARMOUTH, HASTINGS UNITED, HINCKLEY UNITED, HISTON, HORNCHURCH, ILKESTON TOWN, IPSWICH TOWN, LEEK TOWN, LEYTON, LINCOLN CITY, LOVELLS ATHLETIC, MARLOW, MATLOCK TOWN, MERTHYR TYDFIL, MINEHEAD, MOSSLEY, NEWARK, NEWPORT IOW, NORTH SHIELDS, PENRITH, POOLE, SHREWSBURY, SOUTHALL, STOCKTON, SUDBURY, SUTTON TOWN, TOW LAW TOWN, WELLING UNITED, WHITBY TOWN, WISBECH TOWN, WITTON ALBION, VAUXHALL MOTORS.

Through the Decades

Decade	Seasons	Giantkillings	Average wins per seasons
1920s	5	23	4.60
1930s	9	38	4.22
1940s	5	17	3.40
1950s	10	54	5.40
1960s	10	42	4.20
1970s	10	75	7.50
1980s	10	65	6.50
1990s	10	61	6.10
2000s	7	46	6.57

The proof is here that the most successful decade for non-Leaguers was the 1970s, with the most disappointing being the 1940s. The present decade is the second best so those who say the gap is narrowing between the Football League and non-League are only partially right.

Other titles published by Stadia

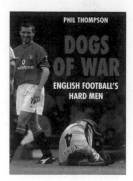

Dogs of War: English Football's Hard Men
PHIL THOMPSON

Throughout the history of football, supporters and players have been inspired by those they consider to be hard, the 1960s and '70s produced 'Chopper' Harris and Tommy Smith, while more recently Patrick Viera and Roy Keane have taken over the mantle. Including tales of hard tackling and head-butting, this collection is one football fans won't want to miss.

978 0 7524 4433 8

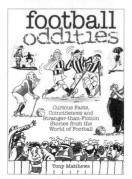

Football Oddities
TONY MATTHEWS

In one of the most individual and irreverent collections of footballing facts ever produced, Tony Matthews has unearthed tales of the unexpected that will delight footy fans everywhere. Did you hear the one about the Argentine full-back who scored a hat-trick of own goals in less than an hour? Read about this – and many others – here.

978 0 7524 3401 8

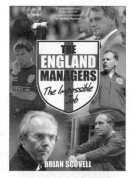

The England Managers: The Impossible Job
BRIAN SCOVELL

From the tranquil days of 1946, when Walter Winterbottom became the first England manager, to the controversial appointment of a non-national in Sven Goran Eriksson, the England post has always attracted frenzied and critical headlines. On the sixtieth anniversary of the first appointee, this authoritative book explores what surely has since become the impossible job.

978 0 7524 3748 4

Seeing Red Football's Most Violent Matches
PHIL THOMPSON

It is a fact that football and fighting are all too frequent bedfellows. This book explores some of the most violent games of all time – every one of them a stain on the character of sportsmanship and the spirit of fair play. Violent challenges, tactics of foul play and ill conditioned manners, they are all here. Upfront and honest, this is a telling insight into the ugly side of the beautiful game.

978 0 7524 3778 1

If you are interested in purchasing other books published by Stadia, or in case you have difficulty finding any Stadia books in your local bookshop, you can also place orders directly through our website

www.tempus-publishing.com